10 PRINCIPLES OF ARCHITECTURE

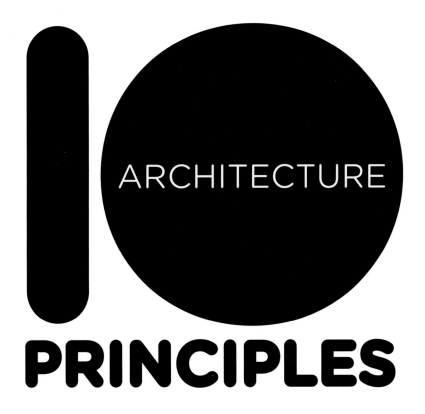

ARCHITECTURE

PRINCIPLES

RUTH SLAVID

VIVAYS PUBLISHING

Published by Vivays Publishing Ltd
www.vivays-publishing.com

A catalogue record for this book is
available from the British Library
ISBN 978-1-908126-28-3

Publishing Director: Lee Ripley

Design: Draught Associates

Cover: Michael Lenz

Printed in China

CONTENTS

INTRODUCTION

INTRODUCTION

The late architect and Royal Academician Sir Philip Powell, one half of the team that designed the Skylon for the Festival of Britain, once drew a poached egg on toast. It followed exactly the form of an architectural drawing, shown in both plan and section, and at one stage the Royal Academy sold a souvenir apron with the design on it. The charm of the conceit lay in the incongruity of using an approach intended to convey the complexity of a building to represent something that most of us can produce without recourse to any drawings at all.

The two drawings provided all the information that anyone could want about the breakfast dish. In contrast, even the simplest building requires a wealth of information. Some clever architects may manage to encapsulate an idea in a sketch on a napkin, but this will be followed by vast numbers of plans, sections and details, almost certainly produced in CAD (computer aided design) and increasingly using BIM (Building Information Modelling).

LEFT
Simple materials, such as the mud used in the Great Mosque at Djenne in Mali, can still result in great buildings

PREVIOUS PAGE
Good architecture does not have to be grand. This house, with its extension to introduce more light, is extremely satisfying

Gaudì's architecture helped give an identity to Barcelona, long before the 'Bilbao effect.'

Buildings are among the most complex objects that our society produces. If you open up a computer you may be dazzled by the patterns of the circuit boards within, but the purposes of the computer are relatively narrow – to manipulate data – even though its potential is so great. In contrast, a building has to keep the weather out, to form a piece of the city, to support itself, and to enable a vast range of activities, from the mundane to the most sophisticated, to take place inside it. No two places are alike, and so no two buildings can be alike. Even factory-produced units will have slightly different foundations.

The architect designing a building has to juggle with everything from the disposition of spaces and the appearance of the façades to the height of the stair treads and the layout of the bathrooms. They have to negotiate huge numbers of regulations and planning laws, and satisfy current and future clients, funders, lenders and users – sometimes the same people but often not. They have to work out how a whole building can be made from a variety of elements, some so large they arrive on special trucks and others so small they could fall through the cracks in the floorboards – if there are any floorboards.

Architects, of course, do not have to do all this alone. There are numerous specialists with whom they work, many of whom are mentioned in this book. But it is traditionally the architect who pulls all these together to create the design of the building, knowing just enough about the topics to at least ask the right questions. And in addition, a good architect designing a building brings to it a special ability – a spatial intelligence that allows them to design in three dimensions and see how to make individual spaces work and also the relationship between them. One could describe a good architect as a jack of all trades and master of one.

So far I have talked about architects, whereas this book is about ten principles of architecture. Put simplistically, one could say that architecture is what architects do. Of course they do a lot more than simply designing buildings. The insights offered by an architectural education allow architects to work in many related fields – as urban designers, as developers, as project manufacturers, as historians and critics. But the heart of their work is designing buildings, and that is what this book considers.

**Getting everything just right
- a house by Tadao Ando**

What makes a good building?

For almost as long as there has been architecture, people have questioned what makes a good building. Precisely because of the many skills and variables involved, this has been difficult to pin down. The Roman architect and engineer Vitruvius coined the trilogy *firmitas*, *utilitas* and *venustas*, most commonly translated as firmness, commodity and delight. Put in simple terms this means that a building should stand up and endure, that it should serve its function, and that it should give pleasure to its users and the wider community.

What is extraordinary about this pronouncement is how well it has endured. Our buildings have changed hugely since Roman times, and the way we live has changed even more. But firmness, commodity and delight are still the three principal aims of good buildings. Vitruvius had hit on a timeless solution.

Le Corbusier's formula

While there have been later attempts to define what makes a good building, they have dated in ways that Vitruvius has not. Le Corbusier, one of the masters of 20th-century architecture, came up with 'five points of architecture' that he defined as follows:

1   Freestanding support pillars

2   Open floor plan independent from the supports

3   Vertical façade that is free from the supports

4   Long horizontal sliding windows

5   Roof gardens.

This is not really an alternative to Vitruvius' trilogy, but a proposed means of achieving it. It is Le Corbusier's formula for achieving commodity, firmness and delight. The problem is that it is rooted in style. An architectural revolutionary who designed some wonderful buildings (even if not all of them were entirely successful), Le Corbusier thought that he was laying down rules that could be used for all future buildings. But as we now know, although his influence was great it eventually waned, and there are many other influences on today's architecture, some from after his time and others from before it.

Skilled architects today acknowledge that there is not just one way to design. They may be firm about the way in which they wish to create buildings, but in judging competitions or awards, they will recognise the strengths in approaches that differ from their own. And we can see the value in many buildings from the past, some adaptable to contemporary uses and others just surviving as beautiful relics.

Dieter Rams' ideas

So the question is, how to take the superb insight of Vitruvius and turn it into some workable rules? I am proposing one solution in this book, but there are many others. The German product designer Dieter Rams, who originally trained as an architect before spending most of his career with the electronics company Braun, defined 'ten principles of good design'. Although they are related to products, most of them adapt comfortably to architecture. Ram says that good design should be:

Innovative - The possibilities for innovation are not, by any means, exhausted. 'Technological development,' he wrote, 'is always offering new opportunities for innovative design. But innovative design always develops in tandem with innovative technology, and can never be an end in itself.'

Aesthetic - Rams believed that only well-executed objects can be beautiful.

Understandable - He believed that products should make their function readily appreciable. A building will typically serve more than one function, but all these should be clear.

Long-lasting - He said that long-lasting products avoid being fashionable 'therefore never appear antiquated. Unlike fashionable design, it lasts many years – even in today's throwaway society.' This is an even more important aspiration for buildings, although many go through a cycle of being fashionable, old fashioned and eventually treasured.

Thorough down to the last detail - Rams wrote: 'Nothing must be arbitrary or left to chance. Care and accuracy in the design process show respect towards the consumer.' Buildings are more complex, and are dependent on the actions of the contractor as well as the designer, but this is certainly a valuable aspiration.

Environmentally friendly - He believed that: 'Design makes an important contribution to the preservation of the environment. It conserves resources and minimises physical and visual pollution throughout the lifecycle of the product.' This is true for buildings as well.

Jo van Heyningen's thoughts

Jo van Heyningen, one of the founders of architecture firm van Heyningen and Haward, provided great insight for the chapter on sound. They list '10 thoughts' on the firm's website (www.vhh.co.uk), in which it tackles the ten values it believes are most important for good architecture. They are:

- Origins
- Sound
- Consolidation
- Weight
- Light

- Primary forms
- Context
- Precedent
- Sustainability
- Materiality

The simplicity seen at the Farnsworth House is very difficult to achieve

What John McRae learned in architecture school

In a different way of looking at things, John McRae, a director at architect firm ORMS, listed in December 2011 on a blog for the magazine *Building Design*, '10 things I learned in architecture school'. McRae's selection was:

1 **Architecture is the 'art of building'.** To date, this is the best definition of architecture I have heard – it succinctly embraces the art and science aspects of the subject.

2 **Every design must have a 'parti'.** My second-year tutor enjoyed challenging conventional wisdom and explained that it is important to have an intellectual opinion or stance on design.

3 **Always ask why?** A key part of your development as a child, this question is also vital in developing design. It is imperative to ask questions from different perspectives to test your assumptions.

4 **Design with people in mind.** One of the strongest influences on my student (and practice) work is Alvar Aalto, who was a master at skilfully integrating modernism with softness and spaces that embrace individual needs.

5 **The plan is the generator, which in turn informs the section and elevation.** A modernist approach instilled in my first year that has stuck with me – a plan of beauty with clarity demonstrates clear thinking.

6 **Computers are not a substitute for thinking.** An important communication tool, but it does not negate the need to use grey matter to resolve complex problems.

7 **The difference between a road and a street.** During a first-year review, Isi Metzstein outlined to a fellow student that a 'road is for cars and a street for people with buildings and pavements'. A subtle but very important difference that demonstrated the need to understand what you are explaining.

8 **If you can't draw it, then you can't build it.** My architecture school had a technical bias and emphasis was placed on the resolution of detail and its integration with other disciplines.

9 **Create a visual feast.** Engaging the user through the senses and, in particular, sight, informs architecture. This can be through scale, proportion, daylight and colour.

10 **Don't wear black!** Dressing head-to-toe in black (and in particular black polo necks) is a no-no. Identify yourself with stylish dress sense and do not revert to stereotype.

My proposed 10 principles of architecture

These lists look quite different, but actually there is a core of similar thinking. The truth is that there are a large number of things that one needs to consider in order to achieve good architecture, and they can be grouped together in a number of different ways. I have chosen as my ten:

> Place
> Structure
> Function and flexibility
> Comfort
> Sustainability
> Legibility
> Light
> Sound
> Surface
> Detail

I hope this is a useful grouping of the ways in which architecture can and should achieve commodity, firmness and delight. If it concentrates more on the commodity and the firmness than on the delight, then it is because I believe that the creation of delight is the true artistic value that sits at the heart of the best architecture. Beauty is easy to recognise but notoriously difficult to define, even less to pin down with a series of rules. But without commodity and firmness, delight will be evanescent or at least short-lived. These are the principles, I believe, that should lead to serviceable buildings within which beauty can flourish at least some of the time.

PRINCIPLE 1
PLACE

PRINCIPLE 1
PLACE

There is a specialist branch of architecture known as 'infra-free' architecture. This is the architecture of buildings that are so remote that they do not have any infrastructure – no access to clean water, to sewerage, to electricity or any other forms of power.

These buildings are often without any real context either – in such remote places that the only aesthetic consideration in their design is not to insult the wild beauty of their surroundings. However they are designed, they are likely to stick out. But what is really extraordinary about these buildings is just how unusual they are. Almost all buildings have neighbours or visual constraints that affect the way that they are and should be designed.

Whether a building is in the city centre, on the edge of town or in the countryside, it will have an impact on its surroundings, and those surroundings will have an impact on it. In some cases, particularly the 'iconic' buildings that were so overhyped at the start of the century, the building is intended to make, or remake, the place all on its own. Others, which are less assertive, work harder to establish a relationship with their neighbours. One wants key civic buildings to be obvious, whether they are a town hall or an arts building or a neighbourhood school. Such buildings have statements to make about their importance and they also need to stand out so that people who rarely visit can find them easily. Other buildings, such as offices and homes, do not need to announce their presence so loudly. If they choose to take a back seat, and provide the scenery rather than the star turn, that is entirely appropriate.

ABOVE
Not every building needs to be a star - a common language can create harmony as in Madrid's Gran Via

LEFT
New and old can work together to give a coherent sense of place

PREVIOUS PAGE
Occasionally a building like the Guggenheim Bilbao can redefine an entire city - but less often than many hope

There has been a lot of criticism about the internationalisation of architecture, of the fact that certain styles are just 'flown in' from around the globe, with no relationship to the city in which they are built. But even doing this is a statement about place-making, often a way of asserting that a city is a competitor on the world stage.

Fitting into the environment

One can look at place-making on several levels. It can be in terms of a building that fits in with the general feeling of the place where it is located. It can be a building that changes its environment, for better or for worse. And as well as the scale of the city or town or area of countryside, one can look more closely at the immediate environs of the building, and at how the building changes them.

There are arguments about the right way to approach these questions, but little argument that they are important. Most of us, after all, experience the majority of buildings from the outside. We only enter a handful of buildings each day, often the same buildings day after day. But we walk or drive or cycle past many others, and they all influence our perception of where we live and work. It is the exteriors of buildings that chiefly create our perceptions of where we live and how we operate.

TOP
Nostalgic but charming - this village street in Burford, England, benefits from buildings that share age and materials

BOTTOM
The deliberately different form of this visitor centre in the City of London draws attention to itself and animates a public space

Think for example of the central business districts of many cities and their clusters of tall buildings, each aspiring to be taller than its neighbours. This was a trend that started in New York and Chicago in the early 20th century, made possible by the invention of the safety elevator and encouraged by a shortage of land, and it has taken off around the world. In Europe, Frankfurt, London and Paris all have their clusters of skyscrapers. Hong Kong, another city with limited land resources, became another high-rise place, as have cities that were later to develop such as Taipei and Shanghai. The skylines of such places are visible from far away and they make a positive statement about wealth, land values and financial aspiration. Yet at the same time in cities like New York and Hong Kong, one's experience at ground level is very different from what one might expect. True you can look up at the enormous buildings, and they do affect the light, casting long shadows, but one's immediate experience is of the mass of small-scale commerce that is taking place, from small shops to stalls and itinerant vendors. You could argue that the architect of the building cannot design for these uses, but in fact the cleverest designs make allowance for some accidental happenings.

The towers of Singapore's Central Business District leave you in no doubt that this is an area concerned with commerce and competition

Sometimes a building not only
enhances a place but becomes a
symbol of an entire country

Planning restrictions

How should a building relate to its neighbours? Often there
are restrictions imposed by local planning laws, particularly in
historic environments. These can include height restrictions
(such as the St Paul's height restrictions in London, aimed at
preserving views of the cathedral), the line of the street or the
materials used. In Paris, for example, a city that has a pleasing
regularity to most of the streets, there are rules not only about
the height of buildings and the number of storeys, but also
about the angle of setback of the mansard roof.

Some new housing developments will have 'design codes'
written for them – a set of rules about materials and form that
still allow the individual designer some freedom, but within a
framework that will, the developers hope, create a sense of
coherence and community.

Design codes for new developments, such as this housing scheme near Harlow in England, help create coherence

Even without these impositions, these are all issues that the architect may wish to address. It is surprising how many buildings, entirely modern in design, still echo their neighbours in terms of the height of storeys and the sizes of window openings, for example, creating a harmonious streetscape without any hint of pastiche.

The role of the building

Materials also have an important role to play. Certain materials are associated with particular parts of the world or particular institutions. The City of London, for example, has traditionally used Portland stone to represent the solidity of its banking institutions – the stone has remained, even if some of the solidity has disappeared. Bricks traditionally were fired from local clay, so that many places have their own distinctive colours of brick. Materials such as thatched roofs, rough stone walls, painted render or timber cladding are all characteristic of particular places. Using these will reinforce a sense of tradition; eschewing them will send a very different message.

Climate is a vital ingredient in traditional design, depending on whether the main desire is to keep buildings cool or warm, whether the sun wants to be encouraged in at all times, kept out at all times or, as is more common, sometimes encouraged and sometimes excluded. As we become more concerned with keeping our buildings comfortable while minimising energy consumption, we are more likely to revert to contemporary versions of these traditional solutions. But windows and shading are not only practical solutions; they also affect the public's relationship with buildings. A building with relatively large windows, particularly if they are at eye level and without blinds, allows the passers-by to look in and engage with the users. At the same time, there is a sense that the building is overlooking the street, which gives a sense of security. At the other extreme, an entirely blank and featureless wall feels unwelcoming and may appear menacing.

Some contemporary hotels engage with the life of the street, rather than shutting it away

This charming cafe is in keeping with the quirkiness of the English seaside and a draw in its own right

The architect of Oslo's Opera House has created an attractive outdoor space and a new relationship with the water

Setting and space

Similarly, the permeability of a building will have an impact. At the most extreme, there may be public routes through the building, but with increasing security concerns these are becoming more rare. However, if the building has a large entrance, the sense that one can penetrate at least a certain way before encountering a security barrier can be created. Hotels have traditionally been meeting places, yet many older hotel lobbies have been hidden from the street. Some modern hotels, however, deliberately allow people to see in.

Very simple moves will affect the way a building feels. If it is set forward from its neighbours, or is taller than they are, then it will seem to dominate. If it is lower or set back, it will be more tentative, and perhaps give a sense of seclusion. A building that is set back from the line of the others will create a kind of courtyard in front of it, and if this is available to everybody it provides a new piece of public space. This is another of the concerns that architects are increasingly addressing. They talk not just about their buildings, but about 'the space between buildings'. You can see this most clearly when you look at a 'figure-ground' drawing, where the masses of buildings are shown in black and the spaces between in white. The forms of the ground do as much as the dark figures to determine the liveability and usability of the city.

The European tradition, particularly in Mediterranean countries, is to have relatively narrow streets opening into squares or plazas. These can house cafés, markets, casual seating, fountains or artworks. They are often places of encounter and repose. Some of the most successful cities work in this way, and it is easy to think that this is a universal model. But that would be wrong. South African architect Joe Noero of Noero Wolff, who is creating a cultural hub at Red Location in industrial Port Elizabeth, has worked with the awareness that Africa does not have this model of the square. Instead, for Africans, the street is the place of encounter; so he has designed the heart of his development on a crossroads with relatively wide pavements.

Public spaces can, of course, be places of public assembly and thus may be unpopular with governments. The revolutions that led to the Arab Spring started in large squares, and the Occupy London movement installed itself outside St Paul's Cathedral after being denied access to the privately owned Paternoster Square. This is just an indication that all spaces are freighted with ambiguity. In many cases architects will be designing individual buildings and will not have the opportunity to create large spaces, but they still influence the immediate environs of their buildings. And the building may have to conform to a larger masterplan.

Too many models and computer-generated images of buildings still show them as objects in isolation, often offering views that their neighbours make physically impossible. It is important to remember that all buildings have a role to play in the wider environment, and should be thought about in that way.

In European cities such as Madrid, squares are valuable meeting places and places of repose

PRINCIPLE 2
STRUCTURE

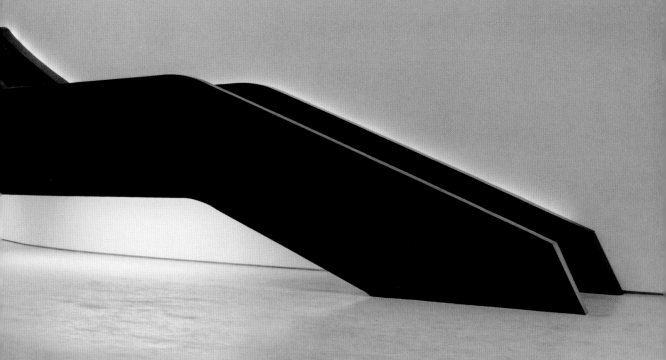

PRINCIPLE 2
STRUCTURE

The single most important consideration about buildings is that they should stand up – and should continue standing in all the circumstances which they are likely to encounter. There have been some well-documented building failures that show this is not always the case, but these often tragic occurrences are, mercifully, relatively rare. A whole profession, that of the structural engineer, exists to prevent such disasters.

Static and dynamic load
Buildings need to withstand both static loads and dynamic loads. A static load is pretty simple. It is the weight of the building itself, plus all of its contents. Offices, for example, are designed with specific floor loadings, to take into account the filing cabinets full of paper that they traditionally contain. Some changes in use, however, can increase the static load considerably. If you were to suddenly decide it would be a good idea to build a swimming pool on the roof, you would need to check whether your existing structure could support the extra load.

Clever geometry makes it possible to cover an existing space like this one in the Smithsonian Institute, Washington

A dynamic load is one that is not present all the time, and that acts with varying strengths and from varying directions. The most common dynamic load is wind. This is a tricky one as it is asymmetric, meaning that there is a rise in pressure on the side from which the wind blows and a drop on the other side. Tables for wind loads are published, taking into account geography and height. These tables deal with probability, so that a 'once in a year' wind is likely to happen once every year, and 'once in a hundred' every hundred years. But there is no guarantee that the one in a hundred event will not happen tomorrow. Plus, with climate change, extreme events are becoming more common.

Vibrations, of which earthquakes are the most dramatic, are also important, as are snow loads that may also build up in an asymmetric manner, depending on the wind. Thermal loads can also be important – as one side of a building heats up and expands in the sun, there will be twisting forces which the structure must resist.

In addition, buildings must be able to withstand unusual circumstances, such as vehicle impact or fire. They may need to be repaired or even demolished afterwards but, as with earthquakes, they should protect life during the event itself.

Getting the foundation right

And it is not just what one sees above ground that is important – getting the foundation right is vital and is the subject of an entire discipline, known as ground engineering. It is essential to understand not only the loads and how they are applied, but also the physical properties of the soil.

The fundamental calculations to work out the structural requirements on buildings have not changed over the centuries, but the tools that are available to do so have developed enormously, and this has had an impact on the kind of structures that it is possible to design. Some of this change comes through a better understanding of materials, but most of it is as a result of better techniques of computation.

It is not that difficult to calculate how much load a particular element of a building can support – you only need to know the fundamental properties of the material and the dimensions of the element, but then it gets complicated. You have to understand how it interacts with other elements of the structure. Even more complicated is working out exactly what all the loads will be. Buildings are complex and there are so many variables, that no straightforward manual method of calculation can come up with an exact answer. Traditionally, therefore, buildings were designed with a considerable margin of error – they erred on the side of caution, so that if there was some variable they had not allowed for the building would still stand up. This has meant that because we are able to calculate more precisely now, it is possible to take old buildings and add elements to them without the need for any additional structure – provided, of course, that we have made the calculations carefully.

In the days before computers, structures were often massive to ensure there was plenty of redundancy in the design

Using computers, it is possible to determine all of these variables far more accurately and, therefore, to make structures that are both more complex and more slender. The greatest advance has come with parametric modelling, which has been made possible with the great increases in computer power. Parametric modelling involves creating a virtual model of a building, in which you define a number of variables. This means that if you want to change one element – for example, increase the floor-to-floor height – you do not have to go back to the beginning and start all your calculations again. Instead the new calculations can be done within the existing model. As a result, you can try out many more ideas within a short period of time.

Choosing the right materials

Advances in materials have also made a difference.
We have extra-strong steel, concrete with special additives
and 'engineered timber' that irons out some of the
inconsistencies of the natural material. There are also
materials that are entirely new – extra-strong carbon fibres
and ETFE, a substitute for glass that is much lighter in
weight and less costly to install.

    Designers therefore have a great deal more choice than
in the past. They can create a visible supporting structure of
beams and columns. They can choose to make the envelope
of the building structural, not just as conventional load-
bearing walls, but in almost any freeform configuration
that they want. Or they can conceal the structure and allow
other elements of the building to be the expressive ones.
Some solutions may be more expensive than others, but
almost anything is possible. One can create huge column-
free spaces for city dealing halls or a series of tiny rooms.
Elements of the structure can be hung from above or one
can create great cantilevers, supported by hidden elements
of structure. It is possible to design buildings as geodesic
domes, a type invented by Buckminster Fuller, or to create a
wilful assembly of odd angles or sweeping curves.

A relatively new material, ETFE, was
used to create the geodesic domes at
the Eden Project in Cornwall, England

Very large-span structures are likely to be in steel or possibly concrete, but for smaller spans materials such as timber and glass are also possibilities. Most relatively rectilinear buildings will have non-structural walls, unlike the load-bearing stone and brick of the past, but there are exceptions – for example, architect Eric Parry used load-bearing stone walls for an office building in Finsbury Square, London, completed in 2002.

Every material has different qualities. Steel has superb tensile strength, meaning that it can resist pulling forces. Concrete, which is a kind of artificial stone, has better compressive than tensile strength. This means that it is very difficult to squash it, but relatively easy to pull it apart. Reinforced concrete was developed to solve this problem, since the steel reinforcement that runs through it confers strength in tension as well. An even more advanced form is prestressed concrete, where tension is deliberately 'locked in' to the reinforcing steel to improve its properties. Prestressed concrete floors, for example, can be made much more slender than conventional reinforced concrete floors – an advantage when there is a maximum height limit imposed on the building, and the client wants to include as many floors as possible, in order to maximise the return on investment.

The Zenith Music Venue in Saint-Etienne in France has a wonderfully slender concrete overhang

LEFT
An ambitious cantilever

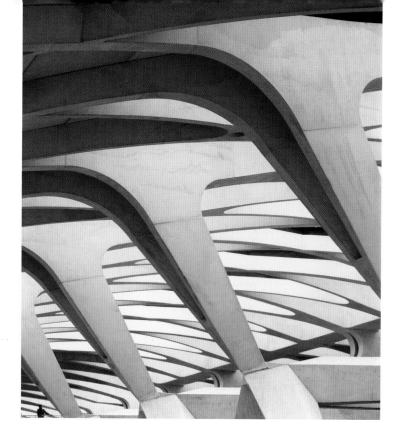

This railway station in Lyon, France, has an organic concrete structure

Timber is a material that also behaves best in tension, and because it is a naturally growing material it has properties that are better in one direction than another. It is strongest along the grain of the timber, that is, in the direction of growth, and this should be taken into account when designing structure. Timber from different types of trees also has different properties. But the biggest restriction has traditionally been one of dimension – trees only grow to a certain height and width, and timber at the limits of those dimensions will be old and rare and expensive. This is where 'engineered timber' elements come into their own – materials such as glulam, made from gluing slices of timber together, or parallel strand lumber in which all the fibres are pulled out and glued together. They can be made to almost infinite dimensions, and with far more uniform properties than the original timber.

Coping with fire

One of the frequently expressed concerns about timber structures is to do with fire. In fact, large timber members will stand up well. Only the outer surface will char, protecting the material within. Providing the design takes account of this outer 'sacrificial' layer, there is little to worry about. Steel is actually more of a concern, since in the very high temperatures of a fire it will lose much of its strength and may not be able to support the building. You can see this in its most extreme form with the destruction of the twin towers in New York on 9/11 although, in fact, it is hard to imagine how any structural form could have stood up to the fire load from a burning airplane.

To prevent collapse from fires that, although serious, are not as severe as the attack on the twin towers, regulations have often stipulated that steel should be enclosed in fireproof materials – a major drawback if the designer wants to expose the steel structure for aesthetic reasons. One way around this is through the use of intumescent coatings. Looking like a normal paint finish, these coatings bubble up in the heat to provide an insulating layer around the steel member, protecting it from the heat of the fire.

Straight lines of a timber structure on a pier building in Deal, Kent

ABOVE
Timber structures can be highly sophisticated, as on this building in Seville, Spain

RIGHT
The traditional English house has its timber structure on proud display

The importance of collaboration

Since most buildings are still built up from rectilinear elements (and rightly so, as they fit so much better with their neighbours, not to mention allowing us to fit furniture neatly into the corners), there will be many buildings that use relatively standard solutions, and a lot has been done to make these simpler. But if circumstances or architectural ambition call for something that is non-standard, it is great to know that almost anything can be achieved. The best projects do not consist of an imaginative design that the architect then hands to the structural engineer, saying 'make this work for me'. Instead, they are a collaboration, with both architect and structural engineer contributing along with other consultants. In this way, it is possible to achieve the most economical structure – which, in a pleasing piece of synergy, is likely to be the most elegant and the least expensive.

Supports for the glazed wall are cleverly hidden in the doors of this archive building in rural England

PRINCIPLE 3
FUNCTION &
FLEXIBILITY

PRINCIPLE 3
FUNCTION & FLEXIBILITY

The fundamental difference between a building and a piece of sculpture is that a building has a function – it is a place in which certain activities take place. It is therefore essential that the building is fit for purpose – a concept that sounds simple, but is actually quite complex.

Meeting tomorrow's needs
The difficulty arises because of the long lifespans of buildings. Most of us find it hard to imagine how we will be living our lives in 20 or even five years' time, yet our buildings are designed to last for 30 to 50 years – and, as we know from looking around us, many last much longer than that. A well-designed building should be able to serve these unknown future users as well as the users of today.

But it is worth starting with today. After all, if a building is not fit for its current purpose, it is highly unlikely that it will suit the users of tomorrow. The first important point is that its fabric should be sound. This means that the structure must be good enough to hold the building up, and it must perform the principal function of buildings in most climates – to keep the weather out. A primary requirement, therefore, is that the building must not leak. With centuries of building experience, it may seem surprising that we have not solved this problem once and for all. Unfortunately a combination of poor understanding, poor detailing, poor execution and poor maintenance results in too many buildings that require a bucket in a near-permanent position to catch the drips.

LEFT
If new uses cannot be found, buildings will rapidly become derelict

ABOVE
A Ming temple in Beijing, China, has become a home and gallery

A former hospital gatehouse in London is now home to a designer

Coping with the elements

Building elements will expand and contract with heat and exposure to sunlight, and if the design does not take this into account, the result can be leaks. If water is allowed to build up, and particularly to freeze and thaw, this will be another potential source of trouble. Buildings must be designed so that they will throw off water. Timber buildings, which can be very durable, are able to resist rain but cannot cope with being permanently soaked. In a damp climate, a timber building needs 'a hat and a good pair of boots' – that is, a generous overhanging roof as well as protection from rising or standing water at ground level, or from splashing.

Most building elements are now factory made – windows, cladding panels, elements of structure – and the greatest problems arise at the junctions between the different elements. If these have not been well-considered or well made, then they may not come together properly, letting in

air if not water. And it certainly has been known for bits of the fabric of a building to fall off – for instance, sheets of glass or elements of cladding to come crashing to the ground.

Another potential problem is with 'cold bridging'. Buildings are increasingly highly insulated, to minimise the amount of heating or cooling that is needed to bring them to an acceptable temperature. But much of this effort can be negated if there are elements that allow heat to travel from the inside to the outside, or vice versa. This can happen where two metal elements touch, or one goes right through the building. Even non-metallic elements, such as excess pieces of mortar, can form a cold bridge.

The high ceilings and abundant space of this former warehouse have made it a joy to convert into a designer's office

Large flexible space in a school

Size matters

Creating a building that is watertight, airtight, without cold bridges and where bits don't fall off is a prerequisite for making it fit for purpose, but it is not enough. Have you ever stayed in a cheap hotel where the ceilings were so low that you couldn't stand upright, or where the room was so small you had to climb over the furniture to get in and out? Those spaces were evidently not fit for purpose.

And if that sounds extreme, then it is worth noting that in the UK, since the abolition of the Parker Morris housing standards in 1980, there have been no standards determining the size of rooms in homes, making the country unique in Europe. As a result, the sizes of rooms in newer buildings have decreased steadily making it difficult, if not impossible, to fit in everything that is needed for normal daily life.

The amount of space that we need, or perceive that we need, changes with time and technology. For example, no hotel now would be built without an en-suite bathroom, yet at the start of the 20th century, having just a few bathrooms in a corridor was seen as perfectly adequate. More recently, bespoke student accommodation was built without individual bathrooms, but now they are seen as a necessity.

Inside whiteboard: jump OFFSITE / GOALS / 1) connect with peers / 2) have fun / 3) escape everyday concerns

The impact of technology

Perhaps the biggest change has come with offices. In the 1990s, with the widespread introduction of computers, the accepted wisdom was that offices needed enormous floor-to-floor heights to accommodate the cabling running through the vast raised floors and large ceiling voids for the air conditioning to take away all the heat that the computers generated. Buildings from the 1960s and 1970s were considered inadequate, because of their meagre floor-to-floor heights.

Now technology has shrunk and we have wireless networks, so we no longer need enormous floor-to-ceiling heights. But another revolution has come along. Technology has made us all so mobile, that we can work anywhere. The only reason to come to an office is not to carry out a function – to sit at rows of desks and perform a task in a kind of white-collar factory – but to see people. The interaction between people, the chat and the meetings that were once seen as peripheral to the 'real' hard work, are now the most important reason for having an office at all. And those changing requirements reflect the design of the buildings as well. Office buildings need many more meeting rooms, some of them enabled for video conferencing, and they need to be attractive places, so that workers choose to be there rather than at home, in a café or even in their cars.

Offices now need to accommodate informality

London's Lloyd's building is famous for having the services on the outside so that they can be maintained or replaced easily

This abandoned hospital in Yorkshire, England, is being redeveloped into homes

Differing lifespans of elements

Another idea from the 1990s, developed by American hippie turned writer Stuart Brand, author of the book *How Buildings Learn*, and by specialist architectural practice DEGW was that buildings should be considered in terms of the five 'S's. These are structure, skin, services, space plan and stuff. The idea is that all five elements are essential to a building, but they last for different amounts of time. Whereas the structure will last for the lifetime of the building, the 'skin', typically the cladding, will only last for 20 years. The services will have a shorter life than that, the space plan will probably only remain for a year or two, and the 'stuff' – the furniture and fittings – may be moved several times a year.

This is not only a useful insight, but it is also important in terms of how buildings are planned. The more separate these items are, the easier it will be to change the shorter-lived ones without having to disrupt the longer-lived elements. For example, you do not want your electrics embedded in your floors in such a way that you are unable to change them without demolishing the floors.

Although this thinking was built around offices, it holds true for other building types as well. Think how much hospitals, schools and even entertainment buildings have changed over the last century. If the buildings that contain them are to continue to function, they have to be flexible and adaptable. And often buildings have actually changed their uses as well. Think for example of the number of 19th-century schools and warehouse buildings that have been converted for use as housing.

**Georgian houses like this one in
London are the ultimate adaptable
building type**

Maximising flexibility

The greatest example of a building type that has lasted and
proved successful in many guises, is the Georgian house.
Almost all of them have undergone some conversion – after
all, they were built without any plumbing – but they have
proved remarkably resilient. Some are still in use as single-
family houses. Others have been divided into flats. Some have
been turned into offices for multiple or single occupancy or
become doctors' surgeries. In other cases buildings have been
connected laterally to provide larger units.

A Georgian building that is used as a single-family house
today is likely to have far fewer inhabitants than when it was
originally built. Even if the family is relatively large, it will not
include the live-in servants who were standard in Georgian
times. This additional space makes new uses possible and is
one of the reasons why designing buildings with the minimum
possible space is likely to be short sighted. It makes sense,
therefore, to create houses that are a little more generous or
to add a little more ceiling height to an office building; this kind
of planning will make the building more adaptable and give it a
longer future life. One of the reasons why people like Georgian
houses so much is that the rooms are well proportioned and
have plenty of natural light. Light and proportion are the bone
structure of a building, the hardest things to change and the
most likely to ensure its continued use and health.

Designing for the future is difficult, of course, because
one is designing for the unpredictable. But it is important for
reasons of sustainability, economy and association – people
like to be near buildings that have a history. Although many
architects have experience working with 'heritage' buildings,
the challenge is to create the heritage of tomorrow. Generous
spaces, rational plans, durable materials and a design that
allows elements that will wear out or become outdated to be
altered easily are the nearest we can get to a guarantee that
today's buildings will be viable tomorrow and well into
the future.

PRINCIPLE 4
COMFORT

PRINCIPLE 4
COMFORT

The earliest American Mercury spaceships, designed by engineers, were not expected to have any windows until architects became involved and insisted that travellers had to be able to see out.

There was no functional reason why windows were needed, they were expensive and heavy, and reduced the structural strength of the enclosure. But the architects insisted, so the windows went in to these and subsequent spacecraft. The spacecraft may not have been luxurious – travelling in the Gemini craft that made ten manned missions in 1965 and 1966 was described as like being locked in the front seat of a VW Beetle – but at least the astronauts could see out.

This is not an argument that has gone away. When the Orion craft was being designed (intended as a successor to the Space Shuttle and subsequently cancelled), there was an argument between astronauts and engineers about the size and shape of the windows. Again, the engineers would have preferred to dispense with them altogether and grudgingly designed windows that the astronauts described as 'like a mail slot'. Most interestingly, one of the astronauts, Edward Lu, told Orion's designers, 'I'd trade food for larger windows.'

Windowless boxes are not confined to early designs of spacecraft. Many low-cost and capsule hotels have been designed without windows in all or some of their rooms. Some create the illusion of a window; others don't bother. Having stayed in one of the latter kind in Stockholm, I must say I found it extremely disconcerting and, in fact, uncomfortable.

A squashy armchair and an open fire typify 'comfort' for many

Comfort is an important issue. It is not, as the word suggests to many, about relaxing in an overstuffed armchair in front of a warm fire. It is about buildings that enable us to do what we wish to do within them, in an environment that does not have a negative effect on either our physical or mental wellbeing. One might argue that in a life of growing stresses and pressures, comfort is increasingly important. Certainly, our expectations have changed.

In 1970, the average indoor temperature in British homes was 12°C/54°F, according to research by the Building Research Establishment. Admittedly this average included spaces such as halls and bedrooms that were rarely heated back then, but few of us would find it acceptable now. Our idea of what is comfortable has changed over time.

Some would argue that these changes have gone too far, that we expect to exist in an 'ideal' environment, regardless of external conditions and of the energy costs and environmental impact of those choices. It is not reasonable to expect to spend winter days in a t-shirt, or to wear a formal business suit in a heat wave. Instead, the pundits say, we should learn to accept a wider range of temperatures, and dress and behave accordingly.

Solar shading can take many forms, as on this office in Hemel Hempstead, England (above), and museum in Boston, USA (below)

Thermal comfort

But comfort is a complex issue. An ordinary thermometer will measure the air temperature, but this alone will not be enough to tell you whether the space is comfortable or not. Purely in terms of temperature, the mean radiant temperature is important as well. This is the temperature of the walls and other large objects. Put crudely, you will feel colder in a room where the air is heated to a temperature of 20°C/68°F if the walls are cold than you will if they are warm. Similarly, on a hot day, you will feel hotter if the walls are hot. If you have ever walked bare-armed past a brick wall that has had the sun on it all day, you will know just how strong radiant heat can be. That of course is the radiant heat from the exterior of a building. Inside a building, the better the insulation the more reasonable the temperature of the walls will be.

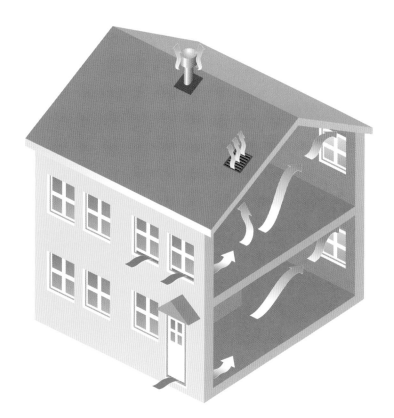

Diagram showing air movement and heat loss in a typical house

Humidity is another factor in the perception of thermal comfort in a building. It is rare that a building is too high in humidity with the exception perhaps of an ill-ventilated bathroom (you can see the results rapidly in the build-up of mould which is not only unsightly but can also cause health problems) or in an extremely sealed building. What is more common, in conditioned spaces such as offices, is that the humidity is too low. Some occupants of the building, for example, may suffer from dry skin or from dry eyes, making it difficult to wear contact lenses.

Air movement is another important factor. If the air moves too fast, one has the feeling of being in a draught; with too little air movement there is a feeling of oxygen deprivation.

Engineering comfort

Building services engineers are the experts on keeping buildings at comfortable temperatures and levels of humidity. There was a time when this would all be managed with equipment – heating to make spaces warm enough, air conditioning to cool them down and other pieces of equipment to ensure that the humidity was at an acceptable level. The only relationship to the architecture would be that the architect would have to ensure that there was enough space in the floor void or in the suspended ceiling for all the equipment, and a decent-sized plant room.

These days, with greater concern about the energy consumption in buildings, the design of building services is far more integrated into the design of the building itself. Just as good architects and structural engineers collaborate on a design, so too there should be collaboration between the architect and the services engineer. Many of these aspects are now in the province of the architect, rather than what previously would have been the concern of the building services engineer. But since the desired outcome is to achieve a particular level of comfort, the building services engineer's input will be vital in terms of modelling the space and calculating the impact of any changes.

Exposing the thermal mass of the concrete ceiling to this library in Brighton, England, is a vital part of the environmental strategy

Improving environmental performance

One of the simplest ways to improve the environmental performance of a building is to use exposed thermal mass. Lightweight elements heat up and cool down quickly whereas heavier elements, of considerable size and made from heavy materials, will take much longer. Concrete is the typical massive material used in construction. By exposing the soffits in rooms, it is possible to exploit this additional thermal mass, moderating the swings in temperature that occur in both the daily and the annual cycles. If night purging is added in summer (the controlled admission of cooling air through secure ventilators), the effect on the temperature can be enhanced.

Some buildings may not have sufficient thermal mass available. For example, in a refurbished building, the quality of the concrete may not be good enough to expose. In such cases, there are solutions available in the form of phase-change materials. These are panels that contain a material, typically a wax, which will change state, from solid to liquid, at the top end of the desirable temperature range for a room. This 'phase change' absorbs a great deal of energy, removing heat from the room. As the material cools down and re-solidifies, it gives out this energy again, warming the room as it is about to become too cold.

There is a wide range of ways to use energy relatively efficiently to temper the environment in buildings. These include underfloor heating and chilled beams in the ceiling. As well as keeping the temperature inside buildings under control, keeping excess heat out is also important. This can be done partly through the use of sophisticated coatings on glass, but also by the use of blinds and shading devices fixed to the outside of buildings known as brises soleil. These also deal with another of the issues related to comfort – the elimination of glare.

ABOVE
Furniture in an office can shift around
every few months, while the bones of
the building should remain untouched

RIGHT
The combination of enclosure and
the ability to look beyond it makes
this space intimate without being
claustrophobic

Human factors

Indeed, while getting the temperature right is essential for
ensuring that buildings are comfortable, it is not the only
factor. We need furniture that is at a proper scale, windows
that are at the correct height to allow us to see out when
either standing or sitting, and stairs that we can walk up and
down easily. If you have ever tried to use a staircase where the
treads were 'a step and a half' apart you will know just how
uncomfortable that can be.

It is often interesting to make more of a building element than might seem immediately obvious. A number of schools and university buildings have included extra-wide staircases that act as meeting places. Some double-height steps at the side also create a comfortable place for sitting and chatting. As we come to recognise that one of the primary purposes of our larger buildings is to enable people to meet and exchange ideas, it becomes increasingly important to enable informal interaction as well as creating formal meeting places.

Perception has a role to play as well. Several studies have shown that when people have control over their environment – where they are able to open and close windows as they wish, for example – they are able to put up with much greater variations in temperature than in a building where the conditions are entirely imposed by the faceless 'them'. Psychologist Craig Knight at the University of Exeter has shown that when people have attractive elements in their environments, such as paintings and plants, they perform tasks more effectively. And their performance improves further if they can actually choose where to place these elements – in other words, where they have a degree of autonomy.

Similarly, there is strong anecdotal evidence that patients in hospitals who can look out on pleasing views recover more quickly than those who have no views or unattractive ones. In the UK, a series of buildings, known as Maggie's Centres, have been designed to provide comfortable, reassuring places where cancer sufferers can go to discuss their fears, problems, prognosis and treatment. In a similar way, the Teenage Cancer Trust has commissioned wards in which teenage patients can feel at ease and non-institutionalised.

Windows that come down to floor level ensure that wheelchair users can enjoy views

Accessibility and sensitivity

When talking about comfort in buildings, we need to ensure that everyone's comfort is taken into account– not just the young, tall and able-bodied. It should include the elderly, the partially sighted, the very small and very tall and, of course, the people with that most visible of all disabilities – the wheelchair user. Regulations are becoming much stricter which means that new buildings must have ramps and accessible toilets, and quite right too. But there are more subtle issues. I once heard a partially sighted person talk about the horror of going into an all-white bathroom with white sanitary fittings, and wondering just where he should be aiming.

As with able-bodied users, design should not just be about making it possible for these groups to use buildings, but also about making it pleasurable for them to do so. Keeping in mind aspects as diverse as the placement of windows or the height of reception desks can make a real difference.

Another aspect of comfort is a lack of fear. There are some daring and exciting elements that can be introduced in design, such as glazed wall-climber lifts and walkways across atria with glass floors. For most of us these add a little frisson to the day, but for someone who suffers from vertigo they will be at best unpleasant and at worst impossible. If this is a building that visitors have to visit such as a doctor's office or a hospital rather than one they choose to visit, it is common sense and good manners to offer an alternative.

It may be that many building users will not even notice if their buildings are comfortable, but they will certainly be aware of any discomfort. They might feel ill at ease, uncomfortable, unproductive or even unwell. Comfort is not an indulgence. It should be at the heart of good building design.

Glass bridges, as used in this office in London, can be dramatic, but there should be alternatives for the nervous

PRINCIPLE 5
SUSTAINABILITY

PRINCIPLE 5
SUSTAINABILITY

Nowadays almost everyone agrees that our buildings should be made sustainable. The difficulty lies in understanding exactly what that means. Broadly, sustainability as defined at a 1987 UN conference means 'meeting present needs without compromising the ability of future generations to meet their needs'. This would encompass such issues as using renewable resources, avoiding materials from sources that threaten the livelihoods of the places from which they originate by disrupting traditional lifestyles, causing pollution, propping up repressive regimes, or exploiting workers as well as ensuring that the building's carbon emissions are as low as possible.

By refurbishing rather than replacing this building in Birmingham, England, the architect has saved a considerable amount of embodied carbon

There are many aspects of sustainability and, even if you decide you want to address all of them, the problem is that buildings are complex assemblies of different elements. There will always be a series of factors to balance. For example, if you put a building in a business park in the middle of nowhere, it will be possible to align it perfectly to make the most of the sun and to have windows that open because there will be very little noise. It will not, however, be possible for most users of the building to reach it by public transport or to walk or cycle there. Almost everyone will have to drive. Studies show that the overall carbon footprint of a super-green building in such a location will be greater than for a less-than-ideal building in a city centre well served by public transport.

This house in Vienna, Austria, was designed to have the best possible relationship with sunlight

Reducing our carbon footprint

In the UK, buildings are responsible for around one-third of the total carbon emissions, so it is essential that this figure be cut dramatically if we are to reduce our carbon footprint to acceptable levels. There are two categories of emissions for which buildings are responsible– the energy that is consumed in use, which includes everything from heating and lighting to maintenance and replacement of elements, and the embodied energy. This is the energy that is involved in extracting and refining the raw materials, in making components, transporting them, assembling them and ultimately demolishing them and either disposing of them or recycling them.

Initially, concern was mostly about the energy that was consumed in use by buildings as, over a building's lifetime, it far outweighed the embodied energy. But as our buildings become more efficient and less energy hungry, the embodied energy, while not increasing in absolute terms, becomes more important in relative terms. It is, therefore, an aspect that is being given greater consideration, both in the design of new buildings and in deciding whether to retain entire buildings or parts of buildings, rather than demolishing and replacing them.

This hotel in Shanghai, China, has
been designed to be carbon-neutral

This nursery in Horsholm, Denmark, combines photovoltaics with a green roof

Terminology can be confusing as well. We talk about 'carbon' and 'carbon dioxide' and then about 'energy'. What we are really interested in is the amount of carbon dioxide – the primary although not the most potent greenhouse gas – that is emitted. Anything that consumes energy from fossil fuels will generate carbon dioxide, although some fuels are worse offenders than others. Coal for example, generates more carbon dioxide per unit of energy than gas does. This becomes particularly tricky when one is looking at the embodied carbon dioxide (embodied energy is just a shorthand term) of a building component since one needs to know what kind of energy was used in its production.

Different types of sustainability

Another problem is that we tend to look at the energy consumption of buildings as shorthand for all aspects of sustainability. In some cases this is legitimate – for instance, the water used in buildings is closely tied up with energy, because of the energy that goes into purifying and transporting our water. But other areas are less closely linked such as choosing not to use wood sourced from endangered forests, for example.

Social sustainability is concerned with the impact that a building has on its community and the role that building plays within it. A building can have a positive social impact by serving as a gathering place for the community or its presence can divide a community. In some cases sustainability factors are concerned with the health of people using the building, with designers avoiding any materials that give off volatile gases that could affect, in particular, the very young and those with allergies or breathing difficulties.

Set on an 'environmentally conscious' business park in High Wycombe, England, this building scored BREEAM Excellent in the offices category

Then there is the term zero-carbon that refers to the ideal that a building should have a neutral impact on the environment. In the UK, the government has stated that all new homes should be zero carbon by 2016, with other building types following suit shortly afterwards. A zero carbon building is one that, in net terms, adds nothing to the world's level of CO_2. This means, since some CO_2 will be created in making and operating the building, it must generate more energy than it consumes, exporting the surplus to balance its carbon consumption. There are arguments about whether the consumption of the building is calculated as just its base load (heating, lighting, etc) or whether it also includes appliances used within it, such as computers, televisions and phone chargers.

Finding solutions

While sustainable practice may seem to be a complicated morass, the question is: is it worth trying? The answer is definitely yes. An imperfect solution is, after all, better than not trying. In the long run, architects will be driven by increasingly strict regulation as well as owners' desires to score highly on assessment schemes such as the British BREEAM or American LEED which offer third-party verification that a building has been designed and built with environmental and sustainability factors at the forefront. Like any scheme that involves ticking boxes, these are open to abuse, but they are fundamentally sound.

But rather than just reacting to a set of requirements, it is worth looking at the fundamentals of sustainable design. The most obvious signs of green buildings are the presence of renewables, in particular photovoltaic or solar panels and, to a lesser degree, wind turbines. In fact, these should be the last elements to consider, not the first.

In terms of energy performance, the first essential is that the building should be well insulated and well sealed, so that its energy requirements are as low as possible. Issues such as orientation, use of thermal mass and exclusion of unwanted heat, as discussed in the chapter on comfort, are also essential. Low energy demand will result from a combination of good design, sound specification and good practice in construction.

Next comes the specification of equipment to be used within the building. This should use as little energy as possible – the best-performing boilers and heating systems, effective appliances and bathroom elements that minimise water usage.

This nature centre in Nottinghamshire, England, uses carefully sourced materials and has a heat pump and solar hot-water panels

Wind turbines are much more effective on a large scale than on individual buidlings

Alternative energy sources

Only once the base demand has been driven down, is it worth looking at renewables. Unless the building is very large and located in relatively open countryside, wind energy is rarely worthwhile on a single building scale. Small turbines have a pitifully small output, and the turbulence found in cities will render all generators virtually useless. Photovoltaic panels for generating electricity are a better prospect. They are falling in price and increasing in performance, but they must be orientated properly (somewhere between southwest and southeast) and not be overshadowed.

Solar thermal, a relatively simple method of using the sun's heat to warm water, is another attractive approach. Like photovoltaics, these panels are placed on the roof. Other systems are less visible. Air-source and ground-source heat pumps run like refrigerators in reverse. Instead of using a compressor to extract heat from the refrigerator and expel it to the outside world, the heat pump's compressor takes heat out of the ground or the air and 'expels' it into the building's heating system. Heat pumps do consume some electricity, but have a 'multiplier' effect that generates more energy than they consume.

Other approaches, such as biomass boilers, which burn wood pellets, can be tricky. There are possible problems with supply (a lot of bulky lorry trips into city centres, for example), maintenance and the true sustainability of the source material. Biomass boilers also need to be kept running almost continually, which means that they may be producing heat that is not needed for much of the year.

There is a similar problem with combined heat and power that uses the waste energy from electricity generation to heat either space or hot water – or both. This system is more effective on an area-wide scale rather than for a single building, unless that building is very big. Our increasingly efficient buildings, however, don't need all that much heat for a good part of the year.

Combined heat and power is not the only technology that works better on a larger scale. Wind power, as discussed above, does as well. Because of the way that the various assessment schemes are scored, generating power on a building-by-building basis is attractive, but is frequently not the best solution.

Photovoltaic panels on a housing project in Nottingham, England

Living roofs

Systems that are effective for individual buildings are those that deal with water. Rainwater harvesting (collecting rain from the roof and using it to flush toilets) is an attractive option, as is the re-use of grey water (water from washing machines and sinks) for either toilet flushing or irrigation of gardens and landscape.

One of the most attractive and environmentally friendly things you can create on a building is a green roof, also known as a living roof. This is a roof on which plants grow – anything from an off-the-shelf sedum mat to a full-scale intensive roof garden, or even a 'brown roof' on which local native plants are allowed to seed themselves naturally. This type of roof has the advantage of supporting biodiversity, especially if you are using native species, by providing a habitat for birds, spiders and insects. In addition, a city with enough green roofs will be cooler than one without as the non-reflective roofs reduce the 'urban heat island' effect, which makes cities hotter than their surroundings. Green roofs also keep the buildings that they protect warmer in winter and cooler in summer – an insulating effect that is accentuated by the presence of water that will evaporate in hot weather.

Another advantage is that the roof will hold water, so that in a sudden downpour there will be less immediate run-off to flood the drains. In some circumstances, this actually allows the drainage system to be reduced in scale. There is a psychological advantage as well. People feel better when they can see growing things. Even if there is no access to the roof for the building users, occupiers may look down on it from a higher part of the building and it may be visible from surrounding buildings.

Turf roofs are a traditional form of construction in northern countries like Iceland

This housing project in London pioneered the use of cross-laminated timber for such a tall building. The 'locked-in' carbon countered a requirement to install renewables

Balancing the choice of building materials

The choice of materials for a building is tricky if you want to make it as sustainable as possible. The first thing to remember is that the materials you use in large quantities are the ones you should be most concerned with – the structure and the cladding, rather than the light switches. Makers of the major materials can provide a wealth of information, and many have carried out life cycle analyses in which they look at all the complex factors that affect their material. These are sophisticated documents, however, and organisations are not above quoting from them selectively in order to make their point. It is worth remembering that if impacts are given per unit of weight, not all materials will be used at the same weight. On cladding, for example, surface area is a more reasonable measure.

Part of the life cycle analysis should include the amount of time that a component will last. For instance, if one component has twice the embodied energy of another but will last 30 years in contrast to just 10 years, then the longer lasting component will have a lower environmental impact in the long term.

This warehouse building in Leeds, England, was refurbished and found a new use

Of the main materials available, timber is the only one that can actually 'lock up' carbon, since it absorbs carbon dioxide as it grows. For as long as it remains in a building, that carbon dioxide is removed from the air. If the timber can be recycled, the carbon dioxide will remain locked in. Another acceptable, although less valuable, use at the end of life, will be to burn it. Proponents of other materials, however, argue that only a small amount of timber from buildings has recycling potential.

Steel and aluminium are the easiest materials to recycle, since they can be melted down to make new components. Set against this, however, is the initial high cost of extraction, particularly in the case of aluminium. Phenomenal amounts of electricity are used to extract it from bauxite.

If concrete is being used, it is worth specifying a mix that contains as much cement-replacement material as possible, since the making of cement is one of the major causes of greenhouse-gas emissions. On the other hand, it is a versatile construction material that can add valuable thermal mass.

It is also important to consider how a material has been sourced. Timber is the material that has received the most attention, because of the emotive issue about 'cutting down forests'. There are very strong certification schemes available, and one can be confident that most material originating from Europe and North America has been sourced in a sustainable manner. With metals and concrete, the concerns are less vocal, yet the adverse impact may well be greater.

Reusing existing buildings

All of these issues are largely concerned with new buildings,
yet our existing building stock far outnumbers anything we
may be constructing now. This presents a dual challenge.
The first challenge is to bring as many buildings as possible
up to the current standards of environmental performance.
The other – related but not the same – is to save as many
existing buildings as possible and re-use them. This is
because, however carefully one sources materials and
components, the most environmentally friendly solution is
not to build at all. An enormous proportion of the embodied
energy in a building is in the frame, and even if it is only
possible to save this and re-use it, the savings will be
significant. Anything beyond that can be considered a bonus.

Sustainable design should be as much about retaining
our existing building stock as about designing new,
'sustainable' buildings.

PRINCIPLE 6
LEGIBILITY

The Barbican Arts Centre in London
needed a major rethink to prevent
visitors from getting lost

Incorporating typography within the
building can provide a clear signal and
enhance the appearance

PRINCIPLE 6
LEGIBILITY

When the Barbican Arts Centre opened in 1982 in the centre of Chamberlin, Powell and Bon's Barbican housing development in central London, one of the criticisms was how difficult it was to find one's way around. Visitors struggled to find the entrance and, once inside, had major problems navigating the building. Some audience members would leave the theatre at the interval and, thinking they had returned, would find themselves sitting through the second half of a performance in the concert hall. It was only when the building had a major remodelling in 2004 by Allford Hall Monaghan Morris that the circulation became clearer. There was widespread publicity, much of which centred on the fact that the building now had a front door.

One might have thought that confused visitors would have been able to work out the route to their destination. There were signs, and by the exercise of rigorous logic, everybody should have been able to navigate the building. But we don't operate like that. We are carrying on a conversation or have other things on our minds, and we want getting into and around a building to feel instinctive, not like a problem in advanced reasoning. We want to move without thinking, perhaps consulting the occasional sign, but saving most of our mental efforts for other things. And if we are stressed or ill – in a hospital perhaps, or just going for a job interview – then we need even more help. In some instances, it seems that contemporary architecture has lost an approach to wayfinding that was instinctive in older buildings. Wayfinding is not something that we do just within a building – it begins at the front door, or rather, it begins with finding the front door.

This building in a botanical garden
in Kanagawa, Japan, uses a modern
interpretation of the porch to signal
the entrance

RIGHT
Navigating the transit system in
Beijing Airport is made easier by
good visibility and the presence of
natural light

Making buildings inviting

Important civic buildings have traditionally been the tallest in
their neighbourhood. Think of church spires. They may have
been dedicated to the glory of God, but they also make them
much easier to find. There are simple clues that tell you how
to get into a building – a path leading up to the front door, a
porch of some kind, a door that is a different colour from the
rest of the building. With too many buildings today, these vital
clues have been lost, perhaps as the result of a desire to create
a seamless façade. But no visitor who has to circumnavigate a
building before they can find the way in is going to admire the
architect's cleverness – on the contrary they are going to
curse it.

A clear entrance sends a message of welcome. In many
traditional buildings front doors were of a different material
– a timber door in a stone or brick façade – and often brightly
coloured. Now, with many buildings having a neutral palette
of metal and glass, this may be more difficult to achieve. But
there are other ways to mark an entrance, either on the building
itself or through the approach. A portico is both traditional and
practical, providing protection from the weather.

Having a well-positioned entrance
desk is important

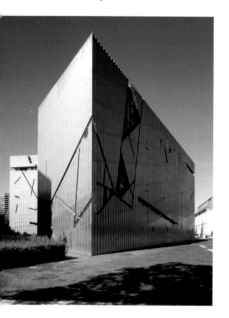

The Jewish Museum in Berlin gains
part of its feeling of menace from
having no obvious entrance

Landscape has a part to play as well. It does not have to be the traditional path between planted areas, but could instead be a change of colour or of texture. It is possible to create 'no-go' areas with inhospitable paving without the need for ugly fencing or aggressive signs. And there is of course a defined language of texture that helps the blind on road crossings.

A building with a well-defined entrance feels welcoming. One can see the extreme opposite in the Jewish Museum that Daniel Libeskind designed in Berlin. It is deliberately intended to be disturbing, and several critics have noted how distressing and hostile it feels from the outside. One of the reasons for this is that the new building is attached to an older, much smaller building which provides the entrance and ticket area. Libeskind's building therefore has no external door – and this is one of the things that makes it so spooky.

Navigating within the building

Once we are inside a building, we still need to find our way around. Few people get lost in domestic buildings, but it is a frequent occurrence in larger structures. Straightforward navigation is particularly important where many of the visitors may be unfamiliar with the place. The position of a reception desk is vital, with its function being obvious. Relatively open buildings, particularly those with atria and circulation running round them, help with orientation. In fact natural light, and specifically the ability to see out of a building, always helps.

Changes of level in a building, in particular where a new building adjoins another, can be an appealing way to create interesting spaces, but can disorientate users. If you start on the second floor, it is nice to know that you are still on the second floor, that the floor above is the third floor and the one below is the first floor. The naming of floors was one of the problems with the design of the Barbican. Depending on which entrance you used, your arrival was either on level three or level five. Most of us feel instinctively when we arrive in a building that we should be on the ground floor, or level zero, or level one, depending on the customs of the country.

Lifts or elevators are one of the most important places to provide signage. Too often in hotels, every floor lobby looks the same, and yet there is no large sign to tell you which level you have reached. An alternative, or perhaps a complementary, way of assisting is to have the lift announce the number of the floor. Not in the manner of one hotel where I stayed in the north of England, however, where the floor announcement was in French. The aim, presumably, was to provide an air of sophistication. It certainly confused a lot of visitors. Similarly, hotels that use names rather than numbers for their rooms can cause problems. It is easy to remember that room 21 is next to 22; less so that Gewurztraminer is next to Bordeaux, which was the fancy of one hotel.

LEFT
The open floors and natural light in the library at Aberdeen University provide ease of orientation

RIGHT
Putting portholes in a door helps with orientation and avoiding crashes!

Providing visual guides

If variations in level – in the section – of a building can confuse, then so can uniformity in plan. If one floor is very like another, it can be easy to forget where you are. This is a particular problem in large institutions like hospitals. One commonly used solution is colour-coding each floor. Often this is done garishly, but it is possible to use subtler colours and still work.

Public art is sometimes derided, but it can help both with orientation and, either inside or outside a building, provide an easily identified meeting place. This may have been more important before the ubiquity of mobile phones, but it is still good to be able to make an arrangement to meet, say, by the statue of the horse to the left of the front door and not keep circling desperately.

Signage should be the last resort rather than the first solution when thinking of wayfinding. This is partly because the less signage you need the clearer it will be. If it is only necessary to signpost a few places or destinations, then the signage is likely to be understood. Even so it will exclude a certain number of people: the very young, the visually impaired, and non-native speakers. Signs should use clear typography, with good colour contrast and internationally recognisable symbols where appropriate. They should also be fixed firmly. There is nothing worse than a sign that turns round, so it is facing in the wrong direction.

ABOVE
Artworks, like this memorial in Sao Paolo, Brazil, can act as a meeting point

LEFT
Colour-coding in health facilities can be subtle but still be effective. Natural light also helps

Meeting the needs of all users

Navigability of a building may be as much dependent on making certain elements recede as it is on making others evident. In one home for elderly patients with dementia, the doors to the residents' rooms were deliberately painted to contrast with the corridors, whereas doors to service facilities such as laundries and staff rooms were made to blend with the corridors. Residents' attention therefore focused where it should.

It is not just people with mental impairments who benefit from psychological tricks. Many airports have garish patterned carpets, but you will not see any with strong linear elements. This is because passengers, distracted by a range of concerns, tended to drift along the line of the carpet pattern, all gathering in one part of the space. Making spaces easy to navigate depends as much on an understanding of human beings as on an appreciation of plans and sections.

ABOVE
Repeating elements, such as airport baggage carousels, benefit from clear and simple graphics

LEFT
Good signage will take the needs of children, some of whom are not yet literate, into account

PRINCIPLE 7
LIGHT

PRINCIPLE 7
LIGHT

The first known use of a spotlight was on the Pantheon in Rome. Built in its current incarnation by the emperor Hadrian in the second century AD, and converted to a Catholic church in 609, it is one of the world's most magical buildings, a soaring circular space with, as its pièce de résistance, a round hole in the centre of the dome. On a sunny day, light streams through this hole and onto a wall, creating an effect with natural light that is akin to the cleverest artificial illumination.

It is a reminder that light is one of the most mundane and most transcendent of topics. We need light to see and carry out essential tasks. But it also lifts our spirits, changes our perception of space and can play a vital role in the modelling of a building. If you want to see just how strong the influence of light can be, look at the work of artist James Turrell, who creates entire spaces, simply modelled with light.

There have been tremendous advances in the performance, versatility and efficiency of artificial lighting. But it is worth remembering that, for most people most of the time, natural daylight is the ideal and the cleverest artificial lighting scheme will only be second best.

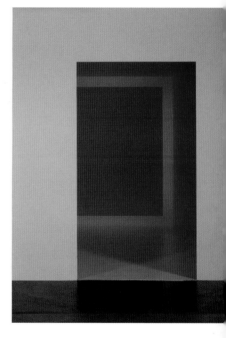

Artist James Turrell sculpts spaces through the use of coloured light

LEFT
The Pantheon in Rome is the first building to employ a spotlight – or at least a light spot

PREVIOUS PAGE
Buildings a long way from the equator, such as this one in Astana, Kazakhstan, can reflect the low sun beautifully

ABOVE
The introduction of natural light into an airport building, as at Barajas in Madrid, is always welcome

RIGHT
The charm of the room comes from natural light and well-framed views, with furniture arranged to make the most of it

Artificial vs natural light

In Hadrian's time, of course, there would have been no artificial light apart from that provided by candles and torches. It is only in the last century and a half that we have enjoyed the revolutions of first gaslight and then electric light, the latter of which allows us not only to see but also to perform complex tasks at times of day and times of year when previously they would have been impossible. We can if we wish have full-power artificial lighting for 24 hours a day. There is growing evidence however that this interferes with our natural diurnal cycle. There are even special artificial lights to help us, for example, recover from jet lag, wake up gently in the morning, or that help children concentrate at school.

These approaches treat light rather like a medical prescription. Most of us, though, have a more informal relationship with light, although we are aware if we are dazzled or can't see to read. Daylight can be both friend and foe. Bringing natural light into buildings is usually a way of making them seem more welcoming and natural, as well as a way of cutting the need for artificial lighting, with its concomitant costs in energy and environmental terms. But it has to be the right kind of light. There is a reason why artists in the northern hemisphere traditionally had studios at the tops of buildings with large windows facing north. This orientation received the most even light during the day, with none of the glare and direct sunlight of a south-facing building. For similar reasons, factories often had sawtooth roofs, with vertical glazed elements facing north, and small sloping roofs between them. Both of these models are still valid now.

North-facing high windows in an existing building form an ideal environment for artists

The changing intensity of natural light

One of the important things to remember about natural light is that its position and intensity changes, through the day and with the seasons, as well as with the weather. The sun appears to follow an arc in the sky (of course we are really moving relative to the sun) during the day, the apex of which is higher in the summer than the winter. These seasonal variations are greater the further from the equator one is, and the highest position of the sun is lower. Only within the tropics is the sun ever directly overhead.

Cleverly designed shading devices can make the most of this variation. A brise soleil (a series of shading bars) placed above a window will keep out the high sun of midday and of summer, while allowing in the lower winter sun. In this way it can minimise undesirable solar gain, but still let the sun in to provide warmth at the most desirable times. And at all times of the day, it allows a considerable amount of light to enter the building, even when keeping out direct sunlight.

Vertical shading elements can be surprisingly effective too. One's instinct is to feel that they are aligned in the wrong direction to have much effect, but in fact, because much of the sunlight arrives at an angle to the window, they can be more effective in some circumstances than their horizontal counterparts. They work particularly well on east and west facing façades, which are the hardest to shade. Putting shading devices on the outside of a building is ideally a better solution than using blinds internally, since it reduces solar gain. Internal shading will keep out the light, but have virtually no effect on heat.

This railway station in Zaragoza, Spain, enjoys daylight coming from rooflights that are angled to prevent glare

The Turner Contemporary Gallery in Margate on England's east coast has been designed to benefit from the sea views and quality of light that the artist enjoyed

RIGHT
Artist Antony Gormley's studio enjoys
north light from a sawtooth roof

BELOW
This Chicago house has a brickwork
screen through which the light filters

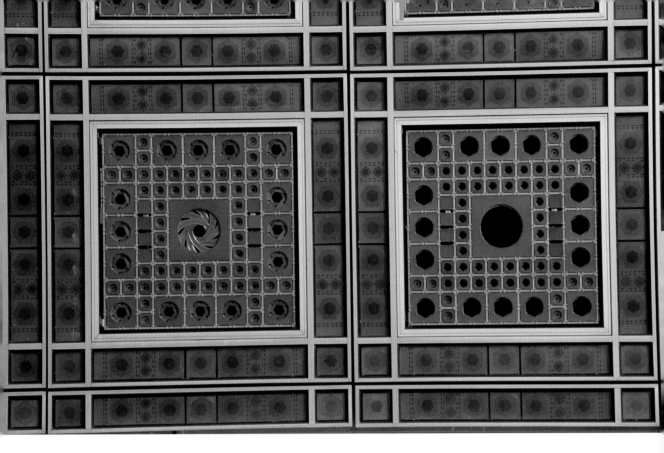

External screening does not have to be simply vertical or horizontal. The mashrabiya or latticework screens that were developed in the Arab world used intricate geometric patterns to provide shading that was both effective and cast beautiful patterns into the building. They provided some ventilation while still preserving the privacy of the people behind the screens. Variations on this idea have been used by Foster and Partners at the Masdar Institute Campus in Abu Dhabi. French architect Jean Nouvel used a more sophisticated version of this approach on the Institut du Monde Arabe in Paris, completed in 1987. There, metal screens on the front of the building were designed to open and shut in response to sunlight, rather like the shutters of a camera. Although undeniably beautiful, they do not always work.

More recently, American inventor Chuck Hoberman has been working with international engineering practice Buro Happold on the Adaptive Buildings Initiative, a way of creating mechanised external screens that can open and close in intriguing ways in response to the level of sunlight.

The Institut du Monde Arabe in Paris has a shading system based on a mashrabiya screen which opens like a camera aperture

TOP
Roof lights can be features in
themselves as at the Scottish
Parliament

TOP RIGHT
The sharp lines of this housing in
Ruedos de Consolacion in Spain are
set off by strong light

ABOVE
A fritted roof light cuts down glare

RIGHT
The deep overhangs on this
auditorium in Leon, Spain, both
protect from the sun and provide
beautiful modelling of the facade
with shadow

Creating more light

Light does not only enter buildings through windows.
Skylights or roof lights are a good way of introducing light
into deep spaces. Some countries, such as Germany, have
legislation that requires workers to be within a prescribed
minimum distance from natural light. In countries like the UK
there is no such prescription, but it is a way of earning points
in environmental ratings systems. And it is, quite simply, more
civilised. This is why one of the first moves in the conversion of
existing buildings, such as warehouses, into offices is to add
an atrium. However sometimes it is necessary to keep light
out when it could be a nuisance and this can be done with a
movable shade or with fritting, where the surface of the glass
is painted with a repeating pattern of white ceramic to exclude
some of the light.

It is not only the angles of light that change, according to
one's geographic position. It is also the intensity and nature
of the light. Typically northern light is more diffuse than the
strong light from intense southern skies, which will cast deep
shadows in the sunshine. Architects can exploit these shadows
in their designs. Materials that sparkle in a Mediterranean
light may look drab under a dull northern sky, perpetually
stained by rain. Importing such ideas without intelligent
modification may bear an uncanny resemblance to that lovely
holiday souvenir that looks so out of place in your home, or
have a similar flavour to that thin bottle of wine that was so
enjoyable on a vine-shaded restaurant terrace. On the other
hand there are also special qualities of light in more northern
skies that architects can play with, whether in views out of
buildings or by the special reflectivity that can only happen
with a near horizontal sun.

However intelligently a building is designed to use natural light, it will always need artificial light as well, partly for the dark parts of the day and partly because there may be areas where either natural light cannot reach or where it is not desirable. For example in buildings that display precious artworks strong ultraviolet light is one of the chief causes of degradation, so using a series of baffles to diffuse the natural light or opting for entirely artificial light, which can be used in a way that mimics natural top lighting, are possible solutions. Other spaces where natural light may not be desirable include entertainment spaces such as concert halls and theatres, where the lighting needs to focus entirely on the performance. In the times between performances, it is possible to build excitement with a dramatic lighting scheme.

Powerful and appropriate lighting of sports stadia is essential. This is Melbourne Cricket Ground in Australia

This restaurant in the Royal Academy, London, uses coloured lighting to make the most of existing decorative features

Using light creatively

A variety of 'stage' lighting can work, where one may want a sense of excitement, in hotel and office lobbies, or in restaurants. In a restaurant, however much one may want to pick out architectural features, diners will also need to read the menu, see their food (and find it appetising) and see their fellow diners in a pleasing light. There are very few places, for instance, where an all-pervading green light will be a good idea.

In a lot of spaces – for study, for work or in functional environments such as hospitals – the effectiveness of light will be the most important factor. But this does not mean that it has to be bland and flat, or very bright and uniform. A combination of background lighting and task lighting (lights for specific uses) can be effective, and give building users more control. Many lighting standards were set before flat-screen monitors were in use and glare was much more of a problem. It will be interesting, as work migrates increasingly away from paper to electronic devices that provide their own lighting, to discover how much additional lighting we actually need. Just as people are used to watching television with very few lights on, so we may become used to working at computers with very little background lighting.

Lighting is a complex subject and good lighting designers, who understand both the aesthetics and the technology of lighting design, can make an enormous contribution. Lighting design involves both the nature of the light itself, and the use of appropriate fittings and controls.

There will be occasions where coloured lighting is appropriate, but in most cases we will want white light. Not all white light is the same though. It is defined by 'colour temperature' with, confusingly, the higher colour temperature being assigned to the bluer or 'cooler' looking light, while warmer more yellowish hues have a lower colour temperature. They each give a very different feeling to a space. Daylight is warmer at the start and end of the day than at midday so some designers have created interior spaces where the light varies accordingly through the day, to give occupants a feeling that they are outside.

Sitting with one's back to a window, once considered unacceptable because of glare, works fine with modern flat screens

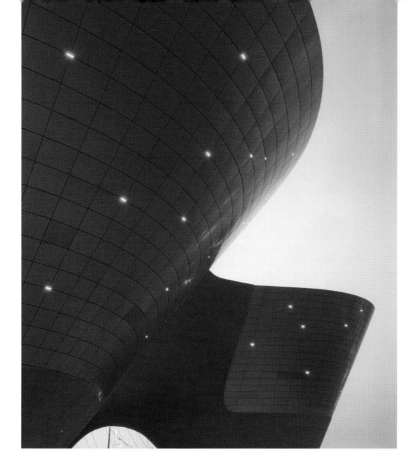

LED technology

The technology of lighting has developed immensely, most recently with the adoption of LED lamps (LED stands for light-emitting diode). These have a number of advantages – they are small, last for a very long time, and use very little electricity. Their use was initially restricted by the fact that while good-quality coloured LEDs were available, LEDs did not provide satisfactory white light. Further developments have meant that a full range of white LEDs are now available. The initial costs may be high, but set over the lifetime of a lamp they are actually low, particularly when you include the reduced energy consumption. The long life of the lamps (measured in years not weeks or months) is particularly important in large buildings where maintenance is expensive. It also allows them to be used in relatively inaccessible places. However, LEDs do rely on proper cooling to achieve their life spans, and this must be thought about carefully in the design.

The low energy requirements and long lifespan of LEDs make them ideal for use in the external lighting of buildings, which can otherwise be seen as an unjustified extravagance. Well-executed external lighting can pick out the best features of a building and hide any infelicities. Garish solutions, in contrast, flatter neither the building nor its owner.

ABOVE
LED lighting on the outside of building

LEFT
An opening rooflight brings daylight into a space with no external windows

**A coffered ceiling conceals
the light fittings**

Fittings and controls

In external lighting you rarely want to see the light fitting if
it can be avoided. This is also true to a large extent within
buildings. Although in a domestic setting, or in a special
environment, it can be aesthetically appealing to see a
special light fitting, in most circumstances it is better if
it is inconspicuous or, even better, concealed.

Another area where great progress has been made is
in lighting controls. Whether these are dimmer controls
on individual fittings, room controls or automatic presence
controls which only stay on when people are moving in the
space, or sophisticated scene setting, which allow a single
switch to alter a range of settings to suit a mood, they can
increase the effectiveness of lighting while reducing the
energy consumption. It is good not to be too clever. Allowing
individuals some control over the lighting of their space is
important, and they should not feel that they have to study
electrical engineering in order to operate the controls.

The contrast of light and dark

Amidst all this talk of light, it is too easy to forget one of the
most evocative tools in an architect's armoury: darkness. Too
often we tend to think of darkness in negative terms, but a
dark corner in a city can be enchanting as well as threatening,
and darker areas in a building set off the brighter spots.
Cities that are over lit are not only potential sources of light
pollution; they also lose the sense of nighttime which is part
of the rhythm of our diurnal cycle. Similarly, inside buildings,
we need to carry out light-intensive tasks, but not everywhere
and not all the time. We should not forget the beauty of a pool
of light surrounded by darkness that has featured in so many
paintings by old masters.

A pool of light surrounded by
darkness creates a special
atmosphere

PRINCIPLE 8
SOUND

PRINCIPLE 8
SOUND

Many of our first encounters with buildings are through books and magazine articles or by looking at images on a website, so it is all too easy to forget just how important the quality of sound is in our experience of a space. It is not something that is easy to see in the plans and visualisations, or even to understand while the building is under construction. In fact, it is not until it is completed and occupied that you can get a real sense of what the building sounds like and of how it behaves acoustically. If you have ever been in the process of moving out, and stripped your room of all its furnishings, you will be amazed how alien and echoey it sounds. That echo is down to the reverberation time and it is one of the main factors in the sound quality of a space.

LEFT
Long reverberation times create a special feeling in cathedrals

PREVIOUS PAGE
Sound barriers on motorways protect surrounding homes

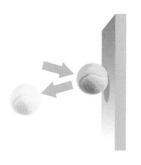

Put simply, if the sound bounces around the room a lot, being reflected from hard surfaces, then you will feel that the place is noisy, and probably have problems hearing. The classic example is the noisy restaurant with lots of hard surfaces, where the noise levels are so high that the diners raise their voices to be heard until eventually there is an impossible hubbub and the only thing to do is concentrate on eating and forget conversation.

Engineering acoustics

Acoustic engineering is a well-respected discipline, with the cleverest acoustic engineers producing some superb spaces for performances. In simpler buildings, these engineers may not be needed or their services may not be affordable. In that case, some simple commonsense measures can be used.

Although concert halls are very special places which aim for a carefully tailored effect, the basic acoustic lessons are also applicable to more general building types. Any surface will either reflect a sound, or absorb it, or diffuse it. Diffusion means that the sound will bounce back in a number of different directions, while reflection or absorption are easy concepts to understand. It may help to think about what happens if you throw a small ball at a surface. If it is hard and shiny, the ball will bounce off (reflection). If it is soft and giving, the ball will just tumble off (absorption). And if it is rough, the ball will probably bounce off but in an unpredictable direction (diffusion).

In a concert hall, the audience wants to hear the music as clearly and loudly as possible, ideally without the need for any mechanical amplification. The kind of sound that one wants varies as well. For instance, if somebody is singing, you want to hear the voice clearly, without too much reverberation, whereas with orchestral music, a certain amount of reverberation adds 'warmth' to the sound as it echoes and gently dies away. This is why some buildings are designed to be 'tunable' with spaces that can be opened and shut off, or curtains that can be drawn across hard surfaces.

The basics are relatively simple. First, everybody in the audience should be able to see the stage, since if the light waves can travel to your eyes, the sound waves will be able to reach your ears. Then, certain shapes have evolved which are particularly suitable for concert halls. One is the self-explanatory 'shoebox' with parallel walls that provides plenty of reflection. Another kind, developed in the early twentieth century, is the 'vineyard', a more complex shape with low dividing walls between sections of the audience, again providing reflection. The design of chairs in concert halls is also a fine art. Often these chairs are designed to respond to sound in much the way that a human body would, so that, as nearly as possible, there is little difference in sound quality between a full hall and an empty one.

TOP
The concert hall in Aarhus, Denmark, is a good example of shoebox design

BOTTOM
The auditorium at Parco della Musica in Rome has vineyard terraces

The office of architect van Heyningen and Haward has been designed to minimise reverberation

Concert halls evolved along with the evolution of classical music. The earliest music was church music, performed in churches and cathedrals, and these typically have very high reverberation times. This is the time it takes for a sound to fade away. St Paul's Cathedral, in London, for example, is believed to have a reverberation time of 13 seconds. Such monuments acquire at least part of their sense of grandeur from the way that footsteps echo. There is a big sound, a feeling that your voice is travelling a long way away.

Architect Jo van Heyningen, one of the founders of London-based practice van Heyningen and Haward, believes that this is one of the few instances where you want that effect. In almost every other building type, she says, you want a far more intimate feeling. When the practice designed the dining hall for Lucy Cavendish College in Cambridge, it was, van Heyningen said, 'the first ever Cambridge dining hall where you can hear one another speak'. The architects achieved this by creating regular openings in the internal timber panelling and putting acoustic absorption material behind. 'A space is almost always determined by its acoustics,' said van Heyningen, 'and it is almost always too noisy. In most spaces, including private houses, people have not thought about reverberation time. It baffles us just how little people have thought about acoustics.'

The practice's own office in north London is in a re-used building, with all the desk work and meetings in a single, pitched roof space. Despite a high level of activity there is an extraordinary sense of calm. This is due, van Heyningen says, to the fact that there is carpet on the floor, and simple suspended sails which are not stretched tightly but curve convexly into the space. Sound can pass through them but

Sound barriers reduce noise
from motorways

not get back, says van Heyningen. And they serve the double purpose of bouncing light back into the room from the uplighters that are used – a further demonstration of the synergy that can exist between light and sound.

Soundproofing

The way that sound behaves within a space is only one aspect of its relationship to sound. There is also the issue of sound travelling from other parts of a building, and of sound coming into a building from the outside. In general terms these are undesirable, although it is worth remembering that if there were no acoustic penetration to our buildings at all, we would feel horribly cut off from the outside world. But if we want to sleep, or have a quiet conversation, or listen to music or join in a conversation or a lesson, it is important that we are not distracted or irritated by noise from outside. Insulation is the simplest way to prevent airborne noise coming in. So good insulation in walls, and well sealed double or triple-glazing units will usually do the trick. For noise that passes through the building fabric, it is necessary to achieve a break in the fabric. So, for example, 'floating floors' in buildings converted to flats will have no structural connection to the elements below them and thus help to dampen noise levels. In extreme cases, for example where broadcasting studios have been placed above underground tunnels, clever solutions have included placing the structure of a building on what are effectively giant springs, which will absorb the sound from below.

Buildings converted to apartments
need good acoustic separation

This classroom has an acoustic ceiling, and opening windows

In the UK very strict regulations have been introduced for the design of schools to ensure that children are not distracted by outside noise and that the reverberation time in the classrooms is sufficiently low. This has not only affected the design of the building envelope, but has also led to the widespread use of acoustically absorbent ceiling panels in buildings that traditionally have used durable hard surfaces. These regulations are in recognition of the fact that children have been shown to struggle to hear in many classrooms, and this has impeded their learning. These regulations are specifically British, but the problem is far more widespread, and many other countries are coming up with their own solutions.

The pluses and minuses of acoustic isolation

Keeping noise levels low is desirable, however one of the difficulties with acoustic isolation is that it removes the possibility of natural ventilation – if you do not want the sound to come in, then you cannot allow the air in either, unless you direct it through a very tortuous route. Opening windows are certainly precluded. But in years to come this may change. Much of the noise in our cities, along with a great deal of the pollution, comes from the internal combustion engine. If we move to electrically powered vehicles, then all we should hear are voices, the occasional slamming door and perhaps, even some birdsong.

This is an important reminder that sound can be a source of pleasure as well as a problem to be 'tackled' in the design of a building. It is a meaningful part of our perception of a place. Think about the difference between walking on a thick carpet or a stone floor, or on a slightly hollow sounding wooden stair – even one with a creak in it, if you are an aficionado of horror films. Each gives a very different feeling to a building and affects our experience of it. Indeed some blind people have learnt to navigate unfamiliar spaces by using the quality of the sound to give them a sense of the size of the room and even of the direction of openings.

The quality of sound is particularly significant in the elements that we touch directly. Just as with expensive consumer goods, a good resounding 'click' can be an indication of quality, so in buildings the sound that a door makes as we open and shut it can be a source of great pleasure and enhance our belief that we are in a good place. Conversely, a squeaky hinge or a dull sounding wall, will make us feel that the space is cheaply constructed with little care.

Sound may be an invisible attribute of a building, but it is a vitally important one.

PRINCIPLE 9
SURFACE

PRINCIPLE 9
SURFACE

The shorthand that we use to describe buildings often refers to the surface materials: 'a thatched cottage', 'a glass tower', 'a concrete box', 'a brick terrace'. Surfaces are the first part of a building that we encounter, and while they have demanding functional requirements, they also send important messages about a building. Are the surface materials expensive or cheap? Are they locally sourced or brought in from around the world? Are they heavy or light? Were they factory-made or crafted by hand? Are they very simple or do they include patterns?

For most older buildings, the external walls play a structural part, supporting at least their own weight and also acting to hold the building up – as well as keeping out the weather. Now we have framed buildings, where the 'cladding' is just that – a covering that serves little functional purpose. Much of it is 'rainscreen cladding' which means that, while it keeps out much of the weather, the real purpose of keeping out the rain is performed by the various plastic waterproof layers behind it.

Roughly hewn granite gives an
unusual texture to this house in Spain

The cladding, however, resists knocks and makes a firm
enclosure to the building. There have been great advances in
the way that materials can be mounted and framed so that
heavy and valuable materials such as sought-after stones can
now be used in very thin slices. Some architects disguise this;
others choose to make a feature of it, to make it obvious that
this is just a 'wrap'.

Cladding with glass

The most sophisticated form of cladding is curtain walling,
which is entirely independent of the main building structure,
and since it is supported by a structure that is independent
of the floors, can span across more than one floor. It can
be all glass, or a mix of glass and other materials. The
all-glass building, seen for decades as the height of modernity

and technical achievement, has fallen in popularity with
the realisation that it is difficult to achieve the very highest
environmental standards with an overabundance of glass.

There is a vast range of different types of glass available.
Coatings on the glass, designed to improve its thermal
properties, to make it self-cleaning or to protect it from bomb
blasts, will all have some visible effect. Reflective glass is
probably the most extreme version, giving a building a blank
rather menacing appearance, as if it is wearing sunglasses.
Even with clear glass, there are different levels of whiteness
and transmission. It is worth specifying glass very carefully.

The rest of the material in a curtain walling system could
be opaque glass, metal – with either a protective surface or a
coloured finish – or stone. Materials may be chosen to blend in
with their neighbours, or to stand out, probably in a deliberate
show of opulence.

Glass does not always have to be flat

Welcome to
Greenwich Peninsula
a place where you can

ABOVE
This college in London makes great use of pattern

RIGHT
Brickwork does not have to be plain

While precious stones such as marble have been exported around the world for centuries – Carrara marble, for example, has been exported since Roman times – more 'mundane' materials such as brick have traditionally come from local sources. They are heavy and expensive to transport. Even within a relatively small country like the UK, there are many different types of clay and hence the characteristic brick type of an area can be seen widely on older buildings in a particular region. Again, architects face the choice of either going with the traditional material or choosing a contrast.

Using bricks

As with most materials, brick provides a wide range of possibilities. Although the size of bricks is relatively standard (and easy to handle), it is possible to choose non-standard bricks. The surface can vary from a smooth 'rubbed' finish to a deliberately rough and rustic finish. You can even get glazed bricks in a wide range of colours. The 'bond' – the pattern in which the bricks are laid – can also vary. The most common is Flemish bond, which alternates stretchers (the long sides of bricks) with headers (the short ends) on each course, and puts the header on one course at the centre of the stretcher on the next. This is a pattern that is two bricks deep, whereas stretcher bond, which is all stretchers, needs to be only one brick thick. English bond uses alternating rows of headers and stretchers. It is possible to use more than one type of brick, to create a pattern.

And this does not exhaust the aesthetic possibilities. There is still the choice of mortar colour, and the option to use special effects such as tuck pointing, which makes the joints appear thinner than they actually are.

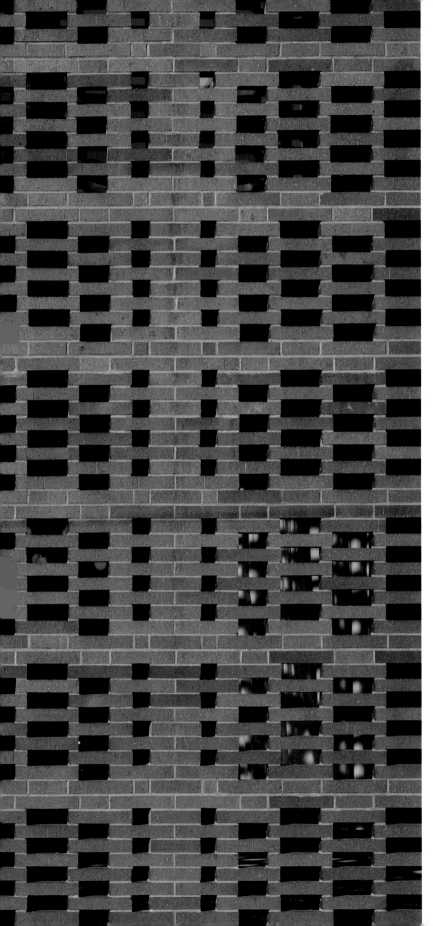

Bricks create an open work screen.
We have seen this house in Chicago from
the other side in the chapter on light

Other materials for external use

Similar choices are available with other materials. You can put almost anything tough on the outside of a building as long as you think about it properly: metals including steel, aluminium, copper and bronze; concrete; other fired materials such as terracotta; a variety of stones and timbers; renders. Some of these materials will remain unchanging over time, particularly if protected from the worst of the weather by decent overhangs and proper drainage. Others will change. Unprotected timber will fade in the sun, and will not do so evenly as it will be related to the amount of sunlight falling on it. Copper will darken and then turn green, but you can buy it 'pre-patinated' with the process already complete. Steel will rust and needs protection, unless you choose a 'weathering steel' which builds its own protective layer of rust. Rain runoff from this, from copper in the process of colour change, and oak that is rich in tannins may stain the material below, and this needs to be considered in the design. The size of elements, the way they are arranged, how they are joined and their textures will all influence the appearance. Some surfaces, such as renders, demand a coloured finish (even if that colour is white), while it is possible to apply colours to many of the other materials available. Wood can be stained or painted, metal can also have painted finishes or have patterns applied.

ABOVE
Weathering steel provides an
intriguing rusty effect on a substation
in Manchester, England

LEFT
Perforated copper cladding at the
De Young Museum, San Francisco

BELOW
Rough stone finish adds texture

A timber-decked roof garden

Even some very old materials that one might have considered obsolete are making a comeback, in the desire for environmentally friendly materials with high thermal mass. So some architects are working with rammed earth (soil with a small amount of cement for stabilisation), and others are incorporating hemp in their concrete. Although these are structural materials, they will normally be visible on the exterior of the building, in contrast to other low-tech approaches such as walls built from straw bales or insulated with sheep's wool.

Before the Modern Movement of the 20th century, all but the humblest buildings had decoration on the external faces. This practice had virtually disappeared, but now some architects are experimenting with decoration again, not in an antique way, but by discovering the effects that they can create digitally.

Consider the roofing

One shouldn't forget that the roof of a building, sometimes described as the fifth elevation, is also likely to be visible from taller buildings or a hillside. In addition, some complex buildings may have several roofs, some of which can be seen from higher levels within the building. Pitched roofs on relatively low buildings are, of course, visible from street level. While the choice of materials on roofs is important visually, how those materials perform will play an even larger role than it does for the walls, since the angle of a roof means that they are vulnerable to leakage. But there are still choices to be made, and you need to think about how materials will look when they are wet as well as when they are dry.

Paving and planting
Similarly, the materials surrounding a building will be
important. Just imagine your costly granite cladding butting
up against some cheaply executed blacktop. Unless building
users are teleported into the building or all enter via an
underground car park, they will walk at least a few steps to the
entrance. As we discussed earlier, how we approach and enter
the building as well as its setting contribute to our perception
of it – either positively or negatively. Paving and planting set off
a building, and need to be as carefully considered as the rest
of the materials. Even a building set right against the street
line is likely to have a small area of surfacing in front of the
entrance. It may be appropriate to make this the same as the
pavement – but it may not.

Rustic materials tell us this is a folly

Marble flooring in this open-plan
living room contrasts with the warmth
of the fire

Choices for interiors

If there is a wide choice of materials to use on the outside of
buildings, then the choices for the inside are almost infinite,
as there is no requirement to resist the weather in the same
way. There may be other challenges, however, in thinking
about what materials to use. Some of them do have to cope
with hard wear. Floors have to resist the impact of feet, even of
stiletto heels. If you look at very old stone steps, you can see
how feet can wear away even the most obdurate of materials.
Along with the aesthetics you need to think about how the
floor will be used. Will people sit on it? Will they get it wet?
Will their feet bring in water from outside? Does it need to be
resilient enough to allow people to play sport? What will the
cleaning regime be? There are also the acoustic properties
that we discussed in the last chapter. Walls will have people
rubbing against them, and in some circumstances will suffer
worse knocks – the rough and tumble of school children, the
bashing of hospital trolleys. Understanding just how durable a
finish needs to be is part of the process of choosing the right
material for the right job.

Carpet is a good surface for sitting on

The tactile and aesthetic qualities of materials also influence the choice of what is appropriate. A few materials, such as polished wood and polished concrete, are so sensual that few can resist running their hands over them. A few timbers also smell good. But most of the impact will be visual. Unless your walls are painted, replacing the finishes will happen infrequently. And most flooring materials are intended for a long life. The choice of finishes, therefore, will determine the look of the space for a long time to come. Not only the look but also the feel of the space will be affected by how hard or soft they are, by whether they reflect or absorb light, and by the choice of colour or pattern, if any.

Worn timber flooring has its own charm

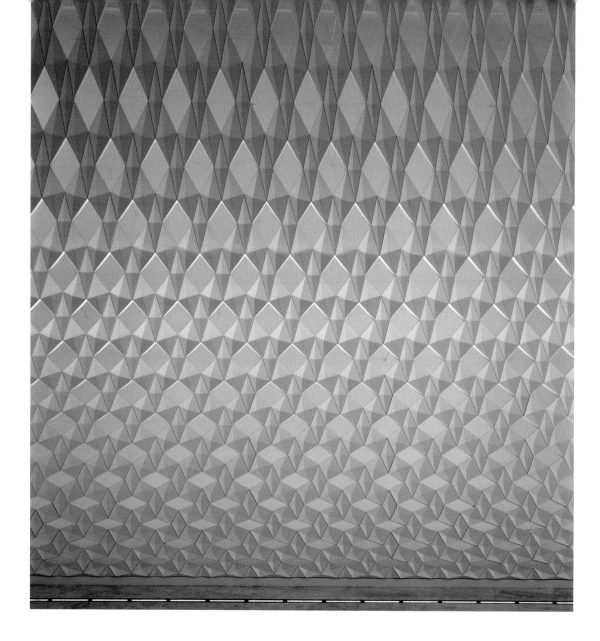

ABOVE
One of a wide range of textural finishes used to add interest to the interior of Oslo Opera House

RIGHT
Marble immediately conveys a sense of luxury

Be forewarned that the selection of interior finishes can be among the most contentious decisions and, because they are among the last parts of a building to be completed, can also be subject to savage cost-cutting. But as many people using the building will spend most of their time inside it, and may only occupy a small part of it, the choice of finishes in a particular area will dominate their impression of the space.

PRINCIPLE 10
DETAIL

PRINCIPLE 10
DETAIL

We don't actually touch very much of a building. As discussed in the previous chapter, we may run a hand over the occasional piece of polished wood or concrete and we may, of course, walk barefoot. But most of our contact is confined to the occasional door handle, banister or tap. We have a closer relationship to the moving parts of the building, and many of our judgements on the quality of the whole will depend on the smoothness of the hinges on the lavatory door or the ease of shutting a window.

These sharp angular balustrades add to the rhythm of the stairs

LEFT
A staircase can be a beautiful object

PREVIOUS PAGE
Well-detailed toilet cubicles will be a pleasure to use

Diagonal drainpipes at the Scottish
Parliament form part of the detail
of the facade

The word 'details' can refer to two things, related but not exactly the same. One is simply the small elements of the building such as door handles, bathroom fixtures, etc. The other is the architectural detailing – the way that two cladding panels meet, or the manner in which the walls meet the floor. On the external envelope of the building, these details may be vital to its performance and durability. Some of the most important are invisible or nearly invisible, either creating the correct pathways for water to run away, or ensuring that there is not a path along which heat can escape. Get them wrong and you may end up with cold, condensation, mould or rot. Other architectural details are more visible, but for most users of the building will not be immediately obvious, having instead a subliminal effect. A beautifully executed shadow gap between floor and wall, an elegant clip, or even the way that the switches line up on the wall, all give a feeling of order and consideration. Ignore these and the feeling of quality may evaporate, although most people will struggle to identify the reason.

Off-the-shelf or bespoke?

Sometimes, it is possible to create an impression that a lot of money has been spent when this is not, in fact, the case. One of the favourite tricks is to buy kitchen carcasses from a large and reliable supplier such as IKEA and then to add new frontages and handles. This is not deception, but an intelligent approach to spending the money where it matters. Because details are, by definition, small, even relatively expensive elements will not be hugely significant in terms of the overall budget of the building.

There are wide ranges available off the shelf, and most manufacturers will produce semi-bespoke elements. In addition, some architects like to design their own special door handles and other small items, which might be created only for that architect, or may go into wider production. It is worth thinking about whether bespoke elements will be available in the future for repairs and replacement. Furniture maker Luke Hughes, who has designed a lot of seating for theatres, takes care never to use bespoke elements of ironmongery on his chairs. However well made they are, inevitably there will be a chair that will fail and need replacement after 15 or 20 years, probably through mistreatment. If the special element of ironmongery is no longer available, it will be prohibitively expensive to recreate it. As a result, an alternative might be used in the misplaced belief that nobody will notice.

Carefully considered fixing clips enhance cladding

The simplest detailing can be the most elegant, as on this Japanese house

Too often though, the failures happen not after a decade or two, but within the first few months of operation. How often have you been into a new building where the lavatory doors sag, or where one cubicle has a replacement lock that does not match the others? The answer to this problem is twofold. First you have to ensure that the ironmongery that is used is as originally specified. There are standards available for ironmongery, but often a lot of cheaper copies are sold. These may look much the same as other simple, generic solutions, but will not have the performance. Often the result will be unsightly and require replacement. In the worst case, such as a door handle that will not open during a fire, they may actually endanger life.

The importance of maintenance

The other issue is to do with facilities management. There needs to be a maintenance schedule for the building which ensures that when elements need to be replaced this is done with the appropriate replacement – which means having a stock of spares or at least information on where to get them. It is particularly important in large organisations like universities that seem to have a perpetual need for new tables and chairs. If there is no coherence and direction in the procurement policy, then there will soon be a chaotic mix of furniture, most of it cheap and badly made. Classic designs will last for decades; on the other hand, there is a reason why cheap items are described as 'disposable'. Taking a long-term view of the budgeting process, it will rapidly become clear that buying quality will offer savings in the long term.

Chairs can be a means of introducing colour

Designing the details for all users

When designing the details with which people will interact, remember that they have to work for all users, as we discussed in the chapter on comfort. Handles should be within reach of children and people in wheelchairs, or there should be an alternative method of opening the door. Pull handles work particularly well because they can be used at a range of heights. Similarly, the physical strength of different groups of people vary so this needs to be taken into account as does visual contrast which is important for the visually impaired.

Banisters on stairs must comply with a wide range of regulations, mainly designed to prevent children falling through them. (The common practice in private residences of installing extra elements to appease the building inspector, and subsequently removing them, is not to be recommended!)

People of all heights can use a pull handle

When choosing items that people will touch, it is vital to consider how they feel as well as how they look. Rounded shapes tend to be more satisfying than angular ones. And there is the all-important question of style. Some very contemporary buildings use a range of minimal details to give an overall feeling of cool slickness. On others, the occasional more baroque detail may add a charming twist. Similarly on older buildings, deliberate modernity may make a pleasing contrast. But there may be details worth preserving for their quirkiness or craftsmanship. The range of solutions is huge – the only certainty is that these details merit serious consideration if a building is to convey a sense of quality and consistent thinking.

ABOVE
Carefully considered storage can be beautiful

LEFT
This bravura staircase is in a high-end apartment in London

Exquisite details, such as this from
Orvieto cathedral in Italy, are often
the elements we most enjoy in
old buildings

These very different handles finish
doors in different ways - but one
yearns to use both

CHECKLISTS

CHECKLISTS

INTRODUCTION

1. Do you really understand what your client's problems and needs are? This includes not only those that have been expressed but those which they may not realise they have. If you end up solving the wrong problem, then however elegant the solution, the client will not be happy.

2. Have you done enough research? As well as understanding your client you need to understand the place where the building will be, its neighbours, its history and its culture – architecture is an increasingly global business, but what is suitable for one environment may not be for another.

3. Is the answer to the problem a building? Your client may do better to consolidate in existing buildings, change their business model or even get a divorce. If you give them a building they don't need, they may not realise it now, but they will at some point – and they won't be grateful.

4. Are you thinking about how your building will work and appear in the future? Fashion can be great fun but it doesn't mix well with buildings that are intended to stand for decades.

5. Are you ready for the obstacles? The client is not the only person with whom you have to concern yourself. There is the planning culture, there are regulations, there is possible local opposition, there is the rest of the building team, and there is the possibility of the client running out of money. Some buildings are very satisfactory and sources of great pride, but they rarely reach completion without some serious headaches.

PRINCIPLE 1: PLACE

1. Is your building going to be in the background or the foreground? Will it form part of the general street scene, or do you want it to be the star of the show?

2. Will a lot of people need to find the building for the first time, or will it be a building that just a few people will use all the time?

3. Do you want the building to look typical of its type – office, hospital, school – or do you want to break with tradition?

4. How is your building going to relate to the street? Have you thought about creating some public space as part of the project?

5. Are you going to design with the materials that are typical of the place where you are, or are you going to use something different?

6. Are there any common features to the area – height of buildings, angles of roofs, patterns of windows – that you feel you should reflect in your building?

PRINCIPLE 2: STRUCTURE

1. Have you thought in general terms about how easy the building will be to support structurally?

2. Do you need large column-free spaces, or are you happy to have frequent columns or supporting walls?

3. Are there going to be any particularly heavy loads that the building will have to support, such as a roof garden or a swimming pool?

4. Is the building in an area that is prone to earthquakes, to high winds, or to heavy falls of snow?

5. Do you want to make a feature of the structure, or do you want it to be concealed as far as possible?

6. Are you prepared to work collaboratively with the structural engineer, with both of you contributing ideas?

PRINCIPLE 3:
FUNCTION & FLEXIBILITY

PRINCIPLE 4:
COMFORT

1. Are you confident that the materials, design and detailing of your building will ensure that it will be weatherproof?

2. Are the spaces in your building large enough to perform its current functions adequately?

3. Have you thought about whether the building will be able to accommodate the changes that you anticipate in the next few years?

4. Is it possible to change relatively short-lived items, such as fitout and services, without having to interfere with the more permanent structure and skin?

5. Have you thought about whether it would be easy to adapt the building to other, unforeseen uses in the future?

1. Have you thought about when you want the sun to come in to your building, and when you want to keep it out?

2. Is it going to be possible for users of the building to open the windows? If not, do you have a really good reason for preventing them?

3. Can you do something else to give the users a sense of control, if they are not allowed to open the windows?

4. Are you using the thermal mass of your building to trim off the peaks and troughs of temperature variation?

5. Have you considered the use of phase-change materials?

6. Have you thought about all the users of your building, not just the young and able-bodied?

7. Can you put in any special touches such as alcoves with seating to provide some intimate spaces?

PRINCIPLE 5:
SUSTAINABILITY

PRINCIPLE 6:
LEGIBILITY

1. Have you made sure that you are giving priority to the 'big wins' in terms of sustainability on your building, and not worrying about a trivial detail?

2. Is the building being submitted for any of the rating schemes, e.g. BREEAM? Do you know exactly what you have to do in order to score the requisite number of points? And can you do it without distorting the intention of the building?

3. Are you using the highest standards of insulation on your building?

4. Are you confident that the building can be constructed in a way that will minimise air leakage?

5. Are all your appliances as efficient as possible?

6. Have you looked at ways to minimise the water requirements of your building? This means not only using low-flush WCs and spray taps, but also looking at the possibilities of rainwater harvesting and grey water recycling.

7. Have you considered having a green roof?

1. Is it obvious to everybody where the entrance to your building is?

2. If you are designing a large building, is it clear where the reception desk is?

3. Will there be clear signage to tell people where they are and where to go when they come out of the lift?

4. Have you ensured wherever possible, that people can see where they need to go?

5. Where you are using signage, have you considered the needs of the visually impaired and non-native speakers?

6. Have you considered a colour-coding system for the different areas of your building?

PRINCIPLE 7:
LIGHT

1. Have you thought about the specific needs of the users of your building in terms of light?

2. Are you designing a shading system to prevent glare?

3. Have you thought about how the exterior of your building will look on a sunny summer day, and also on an overcast winter day? Visualisations tend to show buildings in sunlight, but in many parts of the world that is not all that frequent.

4. Have you looked at ways of bringing as much daylight as possible into the building?

5. Do you really need uniform bright light throughout the building, or could you have a low level of background lighting and some more intense task lighting?

6. How can the lighting adapt to suit different circumstances, such as switching between a boardroom meeting and a presentation, or between an informal lunchtime and intimate dinners?

7. Have you thought about the power of having some areas of darkness?

PRINCIPLE 8:
SOUND

1. Have you thought about how your building will sound as well as how it will look?

2. Are there any specific acoustic requirements for the building or parts of the building? Will it be used for presentations or performances?

3. Do you know what the reverberation times of your key spaces will be?

4. Can you use acoustically absorbent materials to reduce the sound reflections?

5. How are you going to prevent unwelcome sound coming from other parts of the building, and from outside?

PRINCIPLE 9:
SURFACE

PRINCIPLE 10:
DETAIL

1. What message do you want the exterior of your building to convey? Is it one of old-fashioned solidity, or something more contemporary?

2. Do you understand how the material on the outside of your building will weather? If it will not change evenly, does that matter? Are there areas of the building on which you should consider using a different material?

3. As well as the external walls, have you thought about the paving around your building? And about how that relates to the surrounding environment?

4. Internally, do you want to create a seamless effect by having the same materials on, for example, the floors, running throughout, or do you want to break the building up into discrete areas?

5. When selecting colours, have you thought about how they will look on a large scale? And under differing lighting conditions? And in ten years' time?

6. Are the finishes you are selecting tough enough to cope with the users of the building and their requirements?

1. Will the details on your building work? And are you confident that they can be made and constructed as you have specified?

2. Have you thought about how handles, balustrades and other tactile elements will feel as well as look?

3. All moving parts will receive a lot of use – and sometimes misuse. Are they tough enough for the job?

4. Will it be possible to get replacements in a few years' time?

5. If working on an existing building, should you specify elements in tune with the period, or should you go for something more contemporary?

6. Do you have a cunning plan for protecting the detailed elements against budget cuts towards the end of the project?

INDEX

INDEX OF ARCHITECTS

PICTURE CREDITS

Every effort has been made to give credit to the appropriate source, if there are any omissions or errors please contact us and we will undertake to make any corrections in the next printing.

p 146, Courtesy van Heyningen and Haward Architects, photographer: Heini Schneebeli.

Illustrations: Jerry Fowler, pp 72 and 144.

The following photographs are courtesy of **Arcaid Images**; frontispiece Richard Bryant/arcaidimages.com; Adam Mork/arcaidimages.com p 6; Werner Forman/WERNER FORMAN/arcaidimages.com p 8; G Jackson/ arcaidimages.com p 10; Richard Bryant/arcaidimages.com p 11; Werner Forman/WERNER FORMAN/arcaidimages.com p 12(left); Schütze-Rodermann/Bildarchiv-Monheim/ arcaidimages.com p 12(right); Jon Miller/Hedrich Blessing/arcaidimages.com p 15; Natalie Tepper/ arcaidimages.com p 16; Florian Monheim/Bildarchi-Monheim/arcaidimages.com p 17; Markus Bassler/Bildarchiv-Monheim/arcaidimages.com p 18; Diane Auckland/arcaidimages.com p 20; G Jackson/arcaidimages.com p 22; Keith Hunter/arcaidimages.com p 23; Natalie Tepper/arcaidimages.com p 24t; Ben Luxmoore/arcaidimages.comp 24b; Robert Such/arcaidimages.com p 25; Marcel Malherbe/arcaidimages.com p 26; Robert Such/arcaidimages.com p 28; Natalie Tepper/arcaidimages.com p 29; Craig Auckland/arcaidimages.com p 30; James Balston/arcaidimages.com p 31; G Jackson/arcaidimages.com p 32; Nicholas Kane/arcaidimages.com p 34; Fernando Alda/Fabpics/arcaidimages.com p 35; Rene de Wit/arcaidimages.com p 36; Richard Bryant/arcaidimages.com p 38; Richard Bryant/ arcaidimages.com p 40; Bob Skingle/English Heritage/ arcaidimages.com p 42; Richard Williamson/arcaidimages.com p 43; G Jackson/arcaidimages.com p 44; Nigel Young/ Foster + Partners/ arcaidimages.com p 45 ; John Edward Linden/arcaidimages.com p 46; G Jackson/arcaidimages.com p 47; Victor Sajara/arcaidimages.com p 48t; Stuart Cox/arcaidimages.com p 48b; Richard Bryant/arcaidimages.com p 49; Natalie Tepper/arcaidimages.com p 50; Ian Bruce/arcaidimages.com p 52; Fritz von der Schulenburg/Interior Archive/ arcaidimages.com p 54; Michael Freeman/ arcaidimages.com p 55; John Teall Flux Interiors/arcaidimages.com p 56; Christopher Simon Sykes/Interior Archive/arcaidimages.com p 57; Shinkenchiku-Sha/arcaidimages.com p 58; Jeff Millies/Hedrich Blessing/ arcaidimages.com p 59; Richard Bryan/arcaidimages.com p 60; Mike Kirk/ arcaidimages.com p 63; Dominic McKenzie/arcaidimages.com p 65; Adam Mork/arcaidimages.com p 66; Nicholas Kane/arcaidimages.com p 68; James Balston/arcaidimages.com p 70; Craig Auckland/arcaidimages.com p 71t; Richard Bryant/arcaidimages.com p 71b; David Churchill/arcaidimages.com p 73; Craig Auckland/arcaidimages.com p 74; Diane Auckland/arcaidimages.com p 77; Adam Mork/fabpics/arcaidimages.com p 78; Richard Bryant/arcaidimages.com p 79; Adam Mork/fabpics/ arcaidimages.com p 80; Ben Luxmoore/ arcaidimages.com p 81; Tim Griffith/arcaidimages.com p 82; Benedict Luxmoore/arcaidimages.com p 84; Diane Auckland/arcaidimages.com p 86; Adam Mork/arcaidimages.com p 87; Blain Crelin/arcaidimages.com p 88; Adam Mork/arcaidimages.com p 91; Craig Auckland/arcaidimages.com p 92; Martine Hamilton Knight/arcaidimages.com p 93; Hans Schlupp/ arcaidimages.com p 94; Martine Hamilton Knight/arcaidimages.com p 95; Rainer Kiedrowski/Bildarchiv-Monheim/arcaidimages.com p 96; Will Pryce/arcaidimages.com p 98; Martine Hamilton Knight/arcaidimages.com p 99; Martine Hamilton Knight/arcaidimages.com p 100; David Borland/ arcaidimages.com p 101; Craig Auckland/arcaidimages.com p 102; Guy Montagu-Pollock/ arcaidimages.com p 104t; Fernando Alda/fabpics/ arcaidimages.com p 104m; Robert Such/arcaidimages.com p 104b; Martine Hamilton Knight/ arcaidimages.com p 106; Natalie Tepper/arcaidimages.com p 107; Shinkenchiku-Sha/arcaidimages.com p 108; Tim Griffith/arcaidimages.com p 109; Keith Hunter/arcaidimages.com p 110t; Christoph Janot/Bildarchiv-Monheim/arcaidimages.com p 110b; Adam Mork/arcaidimages.com p 111l; Michael Freeman/arcaidimages.com p 111r; Craig Auckland/arcaidimages.com p 112; Alan Weinbraub/arcaidimages.com p 113; Joel Knight/arcaidimages.com p 114; Richard Bryant/arcaidimages.com p 115; Nigel Young/Foster + Partners/arcaidimages.com p 116; David Clapp/arcaidimages.com p 118; Richard Bryant/arcaidimages.com p 119; Anthony Harrison/arcaidimages.com p 120t; Richard Bryant/arcaidimages.com p 120b; Keith Hunter/ arcaidimages.com p 122; G. Jackson/arcaidimages.com 123; Richard Bryant/arcaidimages.com p 124; Richard Bryant/ arcaidimages.com p 126t; Steve Hall/Hedrich Blessing/arcaidimages.com p 126b; Colin Dixon/arcaidimages.com p 127; Fernando Alda/ fabpics/arcaidimages.com p 128; David Borland/arcaidimages.com p 129; Richard Bryant/arcaidimages.com p 130; Richard Bryant/arcaidimages.com p 131; John Gollings/arcaidimages.com p 132; Richard Bryant/arcaidimages.com p 134; Diane Auckland/ arcaidimages.com p 135; Richard Bryant/ arcaidimages.com p 136; Robert Such/arcaidimages.com p 137; Richard Bryant/arcaidimages.com p 138; Ben McMillan/arcaidimages.com p 139; John Gollings/arcaidimages.com p 140; Julian Elliott/arcaidimages.com p 142; Adam Mork/fabpics/ arcaidimages.com p 145t; Richard Bryant/arcaidimages.com p 145b; John Gollings/ arcaidimages.com p 147t; Martine Hamilton Knight/ arcaidimages.com p 147b; Diane Auckland/arcaidimages.com p 148; Philippa Lewis/ Edifice/ arcaidimages.com p 149; Luke White/Interior Archive/ arcaidimages.com p 152; Daniel Hopkinson/arcaidimages.com p 152; Eugeni Pons/ arcaidimages.com p 154; David Clapp/arcaidimages.com p 155; Morley von Sternberg/arcaidimages.com p 156; Diane Auckland/arcaidimages.com p 157; Steve Hall/Hedrich Blessing/arcaidimages.com p 158; Morley von Sternberg/ arcaidimages.com p 160l; Martine Hamilton Knight/arcaidimages.com p 160r; Daniel Hopkinson/ arcaidimages.com p 161t; Martine Hamilton Knight/ arcaidimages.com p 161 bl; James Balston/ arcaidimages.com p 161 br; Pedro Silmon/arcaidimages.com p 162; Fritz von der Schulenburg/Interior Archive/ arcaidimages.com p 163; Friedhelm Thomas/ EWA/ arcaidimages.com p 164; John Edward Linden/ arcaidimages.com p 165t; Perry Masgtrovito/arcaidimages.com p 165b; Nicholas Kane/arcaidimages.com p 166; James Balston/arcaidimages.com p 167; Segev Photography/arcaidimages.com p 168; John Edward Linden/arcaidimages.com p 170; Adam Mork/arcaidimages.com p 171; Nicholas Kane/arcaidimages.com p 172; Dave Cabrera/arcaidimages.com p 173; Shinkenchiku-Sha/arcaidimages.com p 175; Adam Mork/arcaidimages.com p 177t; Morley von Sternberg/arcaidimages.com p 177b; Richard Bryant/ arcaidimages.com p 178; Richard Bryant/arcaidimages.com p 179; Martin Lof/arcaidimages.com p 180t; Mark Fiennes/arcaidimages.com p 180b; Mike Burton/arcaidimages.com p 181.

ACKNOWLEDGEMENTS

I would like to thank everybody who has talked to me about architecture in the past two decades, and in particular Jo van Heyningen for her insight into acoustics and John McRae for letting me borrow his list.